"**ONE FOR THE ROAD** is an extraordinary book – honest, raw, thorough, generous and kind, I think this is an incredible resource, and it's going to help so many people. I love that this book includes such a wide range of voices, it's so moving to know that so many people have been inspired to share their stories. No matter what your relationship is with alcohol, this will give you an important insight into the role it plays in all of our lives."

– Daisy Buchanan,
award-winning journalist, author and broadcaster

"**ONE FOR THE ROAD** is warm, wise, brutally honest and hugely helpful."

– Clare Pooley, author of *The Sober Diaries*

"**ONE FOR THE ROAD** manages to encapsulate Dave's unique and accessible approach to sobriety extremely effectively. Covering different topics, and with input and views from a diverse range of people, this is a highly enjoyable and enlightening read."

– William Porter, author of *Alcohol Explained*

SOBERDAVE

ONE FOR
THE
ROAD

SOBERDAVE

DAVID WILSON

Dedicated to all of you who are struggling with alcohol and sobriety.
I hope this book will help you to find the future you truly deserve.

CONTENTS

An introduction to me, opening with the pivotal week I spent in Eastbourne in 2018, having sunk to the lowest depths of my addiction. Honest and inclusive, as with many of the chapters in the book, it aims to bring a humility and lack of judgement to alcoholism through sharing my experience of how it feels to be in the grip of this life-shrinking dependency. I talk about how this period in my life was the start of my swimming back up from the seabed of sadness, bringing unresolved anger and pain to the surface. This chapter also outlines what I want to achieve through *One for the Road* and how there is something for everyone – from those still-dependent to the newly sober to the seasoned 'recoverers'. Tips on how to approach and navigate each stage of recovery, along with maintaining sobriety through challenging times, and how my experiences and those of my fellow recoverees can bring identification, hopefully comfort and practical guidance to anyone who recognises themselves or someone they love within the pages of this book.

CHILDHOOD 1

This one focuses on childhood experience and how it relates to self-esteem (sense of value in the world), where coping mechanisms might start to emerge, how our younger selves learn to respond to emotional challenges and how in later life we often bury painful feelings from childhood, or take on blame that doesn't belong to us. I talk here about my upbringing, the relationship I had with my parents and the one they had with each other. Coaching on how to view the child you were with compassion – putting your arms around your younger self', and how to balance respect for your trauma with understanding of how others behaved towards you. And the wonderful Johnny Lawrence, a self-development coach whose harrowing story is proof that you can triumph over childhood, provides an insight into the challenges he faced as the mixed-race child of an abusive father.

CHILDREN OF ALCOHOLICS 20

This chapter explores how the experience of having an alcoholic parent affects us, both in childhood and in our adult lives. I explore how the trauma attached to COAs (Children of Alcoholics) is unique, and so often leads to mental health issues such as depression, extreme sadness and a feeling of worthlessness and abandonment. I include a powerful and lengthy testament from adult COA Sarah Drage, whose story may resonate with those who've experienced parental alcoholism. Finally, I give coaching expertise on how to manage and transcend the trauma of being a COA.

THE GENDER DIVIDE

This chapter explores how men and women are viewed differently in society when they drink. I'll discuss how a patriarchal society has long enabled men to pursue alcohol dependence in plain sight, whereas women are subject to different standards and a certain amount of misogyny if they are visibly alcoholic. I'll also explore male drinking and its connection to male violence, the rise of the nineties 'ladette', and whether men and women will ever be equal when it comes to addiction.

ALCOHOL GIVES YOU WINGS

This chapter homes in on that point, generally in adolescence, when we discover what we perceive as the 'benefits' of alcohol. At this time of life, when social awkwardness and lack of confidence show themselves, even the most stable of teenagers can succumb to the 'magical effects' of booze. I talk about peer pressure, wanting to conform with mates, how we try and keep up, and how this period can extend into a long-term coping mechanism. I also share about my own memories of a time when booze felt like a magic carpet, which worked to increase my popularity and sense of belonging in my social group, as well as blunting the edges of my trauma. I explore how teenage drinking can escalate from 'rite of passage' to problematic in invidious ways. Here, Victoria Vanstone, AKA drunkmummysobermummy, a writer and podcaster, tells us a little of how her family's normalisation of drinking meant she wasn't prepared for the dark side of drinking to excess.

GREY AREA DRINKING   86
Here I explore how grey-area drinking is rife, and the most socially acceptable, yet arguably the most dangerous form of alcohol dependence, embedded as it is within today's comedy tropes and memes. I'll talk about how grey-area drinking evolves in both genders, how it is often not recognised as a problem and so can easily lead to more serious addiction, and how to identify and address it in yourself and those around you. And mental health campaigner, writer and superstar Bryony Gordon pops in to share a snippet of experience with GAD.

CHOOSING SOBRIETY   102
This chapter explores the courageous decision to give up drinking, and the vital preparation needed to prepare you for going sober, keeping motivated and alert to the challenges of the first days, weeks and months of sobriety. How self-exploration creates self-compassion and self-awareness and addresses feelings of shame and worthlessness. I'll draw on my own and others' experiences around this pivotal decision and provide practical but motivational guidance and support.

TAKING THE PLUNGE   113

The focus here is on how to manage and keep motivated during the early stages of sobriety. The importance of taking one day at time, building your emotional toolbox, and how to put yourself first by moving away from triggering situations and people (including changing your social setup and eliminating certain relationships). Coaching here focuses on connecting with strength, resilience and a sense of purpose. Again, visualisation – picturing the life you want to have – helps create goals and motivation. I also explore both the importance and the dangers of distraction, and the power of humility and gratitude for each day of sobriety.

RECOVERY: TREATMENT METHODS
AND MEDS   128

Here's where I take you through the various methods of withdrawing from and giving up alcohol that are available. It is a balanced view, though AA and 12-Step was not for me (and I will include autobiographical narrative on this), exploring meetings and mentors, etc. How to find the support system that works for you. How to use social media and maintain good mental health, and the power of being openly vulnerable.

HITTING WALLS   144

This focuses on those periods or challenging situations and events that make long-term staying sober more of a challenge. Redundancy, depression, relationship issues, illness, bereavement, global pandemics, debt, loneliness, Christmas, birthdays, parties. I will talk in detail about my own challenges over the course of my sobriety so far; how recovery is a lifelong process and failure does not have to mean falling back into the grip of addiction. And another bonus: writer, speaker and campaigner Stacey Heale gives us a candid insight into the wall she came up against when her husband's terminal illness collided with the lockdown of 2020 and how she dealt with the trauma of it all with denial in the form of booze.

ADDICTION, RECOVERY AND RELATIONSHIPS 160

I delve into how both addiction and sobriety affect relationships, our sense of identity and how our grasp of a healthy relationship is so often warped, both by addiction and by childhood experience and the very trauma that might have led us down the addiction path in the first place. I discuss the challenges of becoming sober in an established long-term relationship or marriage, the importance of self-narrative for both the addict and their partner, and address the sometimes difficult but necessary choice to let go of a relationship that cannot be mended. I will include my own chequered relationship history, examining the importance of growth and learning out of what is perceived as failure.

ONE DAY AT A TIME 175

In this final chapter, I consolidate the areas of addiction I have explored throughout this book, and emphasise the importance of both visualising the future you want and employing patience in getting there. I also restate the power of community support and professional expertise in keeping you on the sobriety track, and that being grateful for each day of sobriety keeps you grounded and humble and avoids complacency.

USEFUL (LIFE-SAVING) ORGANISATIONS 180

Help is always at hand with the many expert organisations in the UK that deal with both mental health issues and specific addictions. I list those trusted facilities to add to your toolbox.

REFERENCES 184

ACKNOWLEDGEMENTS 185

A NOTE FROM THE AUTHOR

I have been in alcohol recovery since January 2019, after forty years of hard drinking that wrecked my relationships and stripped my self-esteem. Since beginning my sobriety journey, I have devoted my time not only to maintaining my own recovery, but in talking to and gaining wisdom from many others on the same journey. This and my successful podcast 'One for the Road' aims to mentor and help others who are in the grip of this addiction to find their own way back to a full life without alcohol.

One for the Road 'the book' is intended to be an inclusive and hopefully entertaining memoir-manual, combining anecdotal experience, tips and coaching, along with the experiences of many inspiring fellow recoverers. I will cover many aspects of alcohol addiction, its potential contributing factors, the science behind alcohol and its effects on all ages and genders, and the ways in which each of these subject areas can be explored and tackled to set anyone in need on the path to sobriety…

David Wilson

'If my mind can conceive it, if my heart can believe it, then I can achieve it.'

— Muhammad Ali

INTRODUCTION

In April 2018, I woke up in Eastbourne, on the beach. Don't ask me if it was a beautiful day, if the sun was shining, or the tide was lapping gently on the shore. I wasn't there to take in the beauty of my surroundings. The fact is, I couldn't really tell you how I ended up there. What I can tell you is that I was still very drunk, that my bladder was full and that I was only vaguely aware of other people – families with kids – around me. It could just as well have been a desert island, with me – a pissed-up version of Robinson Crusoe – lost, and with no idea how to find my way home. And when I say 'home', I'm not talking about a large semi-detached in Wandsworth, I'm talking about any place I felt I belonged.

It wasn't the first time I'd gone on a bender, there'd been plenty over the years, but it was the first time I started waking up and being fully aware that I was in a lot of trouble. On a quiet, intrinsic level, I knew that if I didn't stop, there was a very good chance I wouldn't be around for my fifty-fourth birthday. On a scale of one to ten of hopelessness, I am pretty sure I scored a good nine that day. Bleary and full of bilious self-loathing, I knew I had to do something. So, I picked myself up, lurched across the beach and found the nearest shop willing to sell me more alcohol.

I'd left London for Eastbourne fresh from another terrible relationship row. I didn't hang around to talk it out, or try and get to the bottom of my behaviour. I just got in the van and drove. It didn't matter where to – just wherever I'd be free to anaesthetise myself without accountability or judgement, to shut out the chaos in my head. Most alarmingly of all, up until then, I hadn't even recognised it as chaos. I told myself I was all right, happy even at times – as long as I kept my medicine close.

The grim details of that trip to Eastbourne are painful to recall. Suffice to say I disgraced myself. At one point I was barely upright, leaning against a wall at silly o' clock when a black cab stopped and a woman got out. 'Fucking loser,' she snarled, and a flash of my future appeared in my head – the soak that passers-by would either ignore or openly berate. I would become like Tony – the guy who used to sit outside East Croydon station in a pool of piss with a can of cheap cider glued to his hand. Glassy eyed. Gone. Past the point of shame or embarrassment. Anyone observing me in Eastbourne – my arse hanging out of the side door of my van, searching for warmth as I lay diagonally in a drunken stupor, stinking to high heaven – would have seen another Tony. Some poor, sad alcoholic with nothing in his life but booze and despair. I was walking that perilous ridge that all addicts walk, where everything is framed by their drug of choice. Life with all its possibility is not in the picture, because all an addict sees is the next drink, the next hit, the next infusion of blessed relief from reality.

You could argue that I was the less dangerous brand of alcoholic. I openly drank a lot and was lairy with it – just your average red-blooded male – though some might call it hiding in plain sight. I compartmentalised my habit too. If I was going out for a big night, I never drank at home beforehand. I didn't "pre-load", as they say. I wasn't the kind to finish off a bottle of vodka and then head out for ten pints. But if I stayed in, it was usually alone. I couldn't be tempted out because drinking 'Chez Dave' was the more hardcore, less sociable yet most powerful part of my addiction. And it wasn't pretty. I wasn't one for booze at breakfast – daytime drinking wasn't really my bag unless it was the weekend, at which point that narrative went out of the window. I had loose boundaries around drinking, and the casual onlooker might have thought I "wasn't that bad".

Wrong.

Alcohol was always on my mind if it wasn't swirling around my system. Though day-to-day you wouldn't have found me slumped outside Tesco with a couple of four-packs or a bottle of vodka, my life was all about waiting to have a drink. I was saved by being vain enough to care how I was perceived by people I knew. I deluded myself into thinking that being in control was synonymous with concealing my addiction. In reality, I was just a more calculating, vainer version of Tony.

When you're deep in the grip of addiction, it's all you have. At least, that's what it feels like. Though I don't subscribe to the belief that alcoholics are inherently "sick", that alcoholism is a disease you're powerless to defeat or that it's a part of you that will never change, I do know that addiction is a tenacious condition that's hard to overcome without a powerful alternative, or a compelling replacement. I'll talk more about the world of addiction later, but for now, suffice to say that in order to stop killing myself with drink, I needed something tangible, something I could use to pull me up and out of the ravine.

That something didn't come for a few months, but at least I had begun to see myself as I really was, and feel the full weight of who and what I'd become, and what I had to fight for. I'd entered into a marriage with a full heart, but without sorting myself out first, and without thinking about all it would involve and what was expected of me. What's more, it wasn't my first marriage rodeo. This one, though, was different, and with someone who had her own battles to fight. I owed it to myself and to my relationship to conquer my demons, but in the back of my mind I feared that my life and its potential was draining away.

When I look back at that time now, I feel gratitude: for touching the bottom of that deep infinity pool of addiction, somehow looking up to see the hazy slideshow of life above its surface and wondering if I had it in me to swim up to sobriety.

Turns out I did.

***

Now, I am a coach, mentor and proud host of One for the Road – a podcast dedicated to ditching the drink. I'm lucky enough to have encountered some incredible people on my journey to sobriety, whose stories have proved invaluable along the way.

My intention with this book is to help you explore your relationship with alcohol without feeling pressured or judged. It's about enabling you to take a step back and examine the possibility of sobriety, and maybe even reframing it as the most rewarding and euphoric act you'll ever undertake. I'll do this loosely through:

- Practical, motivational tips backed up with addiction-focused science.
- Full disclosure on my own experiences of alcohol and addiction.
- Sharing the most insightful, inspiring and, at times, hard-hitting wisdom from my podcast guests and Instagram community: @soberdave.

IS THIS BOOK FOR YOU?

Drinkers are a diverse species. Many have absolutely no idea they "have a problem" and neither does anyone around them. "I don't drink every day" or "I hardly ever get drunk" are both statements that can conceal an addiction, as is "I just have a couple of glasses of wine after work, to take the edge off". If you're of the latter variety of drinker, think about what you define as a "couple of glasses"? Do they amount to half a bottle? Has one glass crept up to two? Do you feel irritable if you don't get your fix in that allotted part of the day?

Alcohol is such a widely acceptable drug that consuming too much of it often goes unnoticed. It's closely associated with celebration, relaxation, fun, reward and good times. But it's also our collective go-to when the shit hits the fan. Something great happened? Have a drink. Something terrible happened? Have a drink. The veritable one-stop-shop-wonder-drug. In fact, not drinking is still largely considered more of a problem that overdoing it, and more likely to make a pariah out of someone. This can be the most challenging element of opting for sobriety, and we'll talk more about it later. But for now, the chances are, if you're reading this book, you're ready to at least open your mind to the possibility of a life without hangovers.

Divided into twelve focused chapters, *One for the Road* will examine addiction and the many factors that can contribute to alcohol dependence, the alcoholic experience and positive paths out of it. Some sections may not be wholly relevant to you, your circumstances, or those of someone you know, but in others you might find real resonance, and discover that you're not alone.

All I ask is that you keep an open mind and be honest with yourself as you read. Take time to reflect on each chapter and hit me up on Instagram with any questions along the way. Going sober genuinely isn't social suicide. If anything, it's the antithesis. You could be about to unearth the life you've always wanted, find your tribe, fulfil all that potential and discover who you really are underneath it all.

I mean, you've bought the book now. What have you got to lose?!

I might just ask you that again. What have you got to lose?

'Childhood trauma does not come in one single package.'

— Asa Don Brown

CHILDHOOD

The twentieth-century poet, Philip Larkin, made no bones about where the blame for our dysfunctional adult behaviour often originates in his poem 'They Fuck You Up, Your Mum and Dad' – but it's a little more complicated than that. Solely blaming your parents for your issues in adulthood is counterproductive in so many ways. It keeps you in a place you don't want to be. A place of self-pity, where you don't have to take responsibility for your own mental health and subsequently stay stuck in that self-created crevasse – trapped, yet comfortable. That said, exploring your childhood, and how it has formed your choices and behaviour patterns, is crucial when it comes to self-discovery. You need to understand what motivates you to do what you do. At the risk of sounding like a cheesy meme, contacting and caring about the child you once were is a massively important part of being a healthy, functioning adult.

One of the great privileges of hosting my podcast is listening to the fascinating and diverse life stories of my guests. The common denominator uniting guests is a history of alcohol dependence, either theirs or a family member's. I am always intrigued to know how, where and why this dependency started, and the impact it's had in the wider context of their lives. Every story is so different, which proves how complex and unique we humans are when it comes to emotional wiring.

My story is one of rejection. My mother was white British, my father native Nigerian ... Growing up in the eighties that [being mixed race] was something that struck fear into people, I think. I was rejected by white people, I was rejected by black people. I remember my mother being spat on in the queue for the post office. She was told she was disgusting because she was in a mixed-race relationship ... So you start to realise you don't fit in. I was rejected from a race perspective. But the big one for me was my home life. I am a survivor of very physical child abuse. The abuser was my father ... and it was horrible watching him hurt my mother, and getting hurt myself. Some of the things I had to witness ... And domestic violence was quite a tricky thing to deal with back then, police officers couldn't get involved like they can now. I downplay the physical violence of that time, even through therapy, because it makes people uncomfortable ... but it affects every part of your life. It's the psychological stuff that stays with you, though, and that causes the PTSD. Stuff like my father would play mind games, he'd tell me he was going to hurt me, but he didn't tell me when. I'd lie awake and wet the bed ...

And when I moved out at sixteen, I experienced loneliness. There's a comfort to chaos and drama and it was gone. That's when I met my best friend for the next twenty years, alcohol ...

Johnny Lawrence – *One for the Road* podcast.

Despite common assumptions, it's very possible for even a hardcore addict to come from a wealthy, loving family with attentive parents and statistically high life-chances. In fact, years later, they might sit in rehab or therapy, wracking their brains for past events that led to their self-medication. And at first, they're likely to come up with nothing – they were fed, clothed, housed, educated – they had everything they needed, didn't they?

Well, maybe not. There are as many different types of addict as there are contributing factors to addiction itself. Affluent, middle- and upper-class kids are just as vulnerable to mood-altering narcotics as kids from impoverished, socially disadvantaged backgrounds who so often fall into gang culture. The nuances of childhood trauma are often hard to pinpoint. Sometimes trauma is so subtle, we only register it as a series of difficult feelings that seem to have no significant or obvious source.

As very young children (nought-to-three years), we are wholly dependent on external forces, most notably our parents. We are moulded by their attitude and approach to parenting, which has an impact on how we experience (or don't experience) love. Some of us might absorb every minor act of neglect or consistent lack of affection and register it as rejection. We can't speak yet, let's face it, all we have is our infant brain to internalise what is going on around us, without the power to articulate our feelings. It's a tricky time for all involved. Whilst the majority of parents actively do their best to provide enough love, security and attention, they're only human. They're bound to mess up. Unfortunately, children can sometimes become collateral damage, which may lay the foundations for an emotionally unstable adult life and a gradual reliance on coping mechanisms, such as alcohol dependence.

Since giving up the booze, I've had to confront some challenging facts and feelings about my past. They were always there, these feelings, but I muted them. Initially, I was too emotionally immature to make sense of them and opted for the usual teenage distractions – football, computer games, girls and then, later on, with large amounts of mind-numbing alcohol. Inevitably, through my rediscovery journey, I've had to recall uncomfortable elements of my own upbringing, as well as some aspects of my parents' childhoods.

THE EARLY YEARS

At twenty-six, my dad was working for the shipbrokers, London Carriers. This is where he met my mum, who was seventeen and worked in the factory there. Maybe she looked up to him – nine years her senior with a steady job. He must have seemed a solid bet, someone she could rely on; he was handsome, and a bit of a joker. Even as a kid, I understood that Dad's role was making Mum laugh. As a family, we'd watch old cine films of the two of them together, young and in love. Laughter was always a defining feature. It must have been a godsend for Mum because there weren't too many laughs in her own childhood – no, not much joy to be had there.

Mum's mum (or 'Grandma Cabbage' as my sister and I called her due to her habit of sitting vegetable-like in silence) was a cold woman. She more or less ignored Mum and reserved her energy for Mum's brother, my Uncle Ronnie, who was an unpleasant bully of a man. No wonder Mum was drawn to my father. Not only was he funny and light-hearted with serious movie-star looks, he offered her an escape from the stilted, unhappy atmosphere at home. Mum must have felt she'd hit the jackpot.

Dad's mum, Emma, was a homelier, warmer sort of woman – I recall a lot of baking. The household was female-dominated, and I often wonder if Dad's constant need to entertain and lark around stemmed from the fact he was infantilised or indulged by the women around him. Whatever the cause, his tendency to make light of absolutely everything meant he wasn't equipped with the right tools when things got serious or went wrong.

My parents weren't affectionate or demonstrative with each other, or us kids. There weren't many cuddles or affirmations, and I never heard the words "I love you". But being the seventies, that wasn't uncommon.

Back then, parents didn't hover attentively around their kids like they do now. We were provided with food, shelter and education and then expected to get on with it. During the school summer holidays, like many other kids of that era, we were often sent out after breakfast and told not to come back before tea. Adult needs came first, and children fitted round those needs. Making demands of your parents was pretty much unheard of, unless it was writing out your fantasy Christmas or birthday present list, and in our family, financially stretched, it would have been very much a fantasy.

I grew up on Aurelia Road, Croydon, in a poor but community-driven area where a lot was done on the cheap – including in the Wilson household. Second-hand clothes and never having the latest on-trend toy or gadget. That was our way of life. I remember when a specific brand of moccasins were all the rage among my peers and I appealed to Mum for a pair, even though I knew my chances were slim. She improvised and bought the cheap "knock-off" version from Dolcis. I kept quiet about the piss-taking that awaited me if I wore them out, that kids being kids, I would be shown no mercy, because I knew she'd tried. In fact, being a "good boy", I felt it was my job to make her feel right about getting it wrong. Because that was my role with Mum and I knew it off by heart. It was only later that I remembered she had enough money to buy herself cigarettes most days.

In the seventies, holidays abroad were a complete luxury, unless you were rich, so we never went very far and even then the budget was tight. Dad would make homemade wine and take it with us to the West Country. Me, Mum, Dad and my sister travelling in an old banger down the motorway. A Bedford van, I think, which frequently let us down. I remember the van blowing up once, the day before we left. But being a practical bloke and fairly good with mechanics, Dad stayed up all night putting a new engine in. That didn't work out too well, despite his best efforts, so we ended up borrowing a car and got a caravan with just the basics. I remember snapshots: sausage sandwiches for breakfast; the sound of rain on the tin roof; my sister Julie and I flying stunt kites; spending long, hot days on the beach making sandcastles; and being held tightly by my dad in the sea as the waves crashed over us.

There were times where things felt stable, we had our routines. Sunday roasts with Dad clanking around in the garage outside, Mum putting the Carpenters on the record player. Me playing with my Scalextric. There was nothing strictly 'wrong' with my childhood, I wasn't treated badly, but I often felt invisible, like what was going on inside my head was of no interest to anyone in my family. If I felt upset or anxious, I had no idea how to articulate it. I kept any painful feelings well and truly inside me, and continued to do so for decades.

I was, and still am, sensitive, which I've come to realise is a gift and not the curse I believed it to be for so long. But the lack of affection, particularly from Mum, hurt me. I knew not to ask for it. Instead, I made it my mission to be as helpful as possible, and to be grateful for everything that came my way. I was shy and underconfident, tidy, quiet and well-behaved, and happiest at home. It was my sister who was the anxious rebel. Looking back, I felt a burden of responsibility not to act up in order to make Mum's life easier. My aim was to address her needs and never state my own.

My sense of worth for a long time was closely bound up with my childhood experience. And my low expectations were to become a defining catalyst for self-destructive behaviours later on in life.

***

At eleven years old, I went up to Lanfranc High School, which had 1200 pupils, and was bloody rough, though it was culturally and ethnically diverse. Coming from the mostly-white Gonville primary school, Lanfranc was a culture shock. On my first day, there was a vicious fight in the playground, when one kid stabbed another one with a pair of nail scissors. I was unprepared for these rough, aggressive peers and very relieved when a couple of years later Mum decided we were moving to Carshalton. I only realised later that this was meant to be a fresh start for my parents. New home, new area.

But to quote the adage "wherever you are, there you go", it was going to take more than a new house in a slightly posher area to fix their relationship.

I was enrolled at Gaynesford secondary school as a second-year pupil. Everyone had made friends and formed cliques, and I was the odd one out. I did eventually make a friend – Adam Turner – a sensible, quiet kid like me, and from a safe, warm family. I was also starting to notice girls. One in particular caught my eye: a bubbly blonde called Michelle. She made a couple of reappearances in my life, but more about that later.

First crushes aside, it took me ages to settle in and behind the scenes Mum and Dad's marriage was imploding. There were clues – Mum throwing a full bowl of washing up water on the kitchen floor in a fury springs to mind – but I was oblivious to what was really going on. I tried to focus on school instead, hanging out with Adam and trying to muster the courage to ask Michelle out. I was going through puberty and, for the first time, my family antenna was dulled, flashing in response to my hormones instead.

I was fourteen when, one morning, dressed neatly in my school uniform, I went downstairs to do my tie and found the house eerily silent, thinking Dad must have gone to work. Then I found the letter on the kitchen table, addressed to me. 'To David,' it said, in Mum's writing. It was brief, to the point and devastating. She'd left Dad, she said, and she'd be in touch when things settled down.

Shocked into autopilot, I somehow got through that day at school, but coming home again meant facing Dad, who was completely bewildered; it seemed to have come totally out of the blue for him. At least, that's what he said, but of course it couldn't have been a total surprise, he just didn't want to see what part he might have had to play in it. Julie and I played along, though it didn't seem real. Surely Mum would be back soon?

She didn't come back, though, at least not to Dad, nor our home, and though we adapted, Julie and I in our different ways, with Dad silently suffering, I never stopped longing for the sight of Mum with her rollers in and a roll-up on the go.

Dad was now a single parent. He fulfilled his duties – coming home from work to make dinner for me and Julie – but he never talked about Mum. While I was still internalising my feelings, my sister reacted with aggression, most of which she took out on me. I distinctly remember her coming home one night and punching me in the face while I was asleep. There was no reason for it. She didn't need one.

Dad tried his best, but he wasn't cut out to be a carer. Retrospectively, I don't blame him – he was obviously dealing with the fact his wife had left him. But it wasn't that long before Dixie arrived on the scene, Dad's new, younger girlfriend, who seemed to be downstairs for most evenings right from the off. I already felt bad enough about Mum leaving, but when Dixie arrived

11

on the scene I felt even more alone. I used to sit in my 9x6 box room listening to the constant laughter and banter whilst looking out of the window wondering how everything had fallen apart so quickly. I mean, now, in hindsight, I don't blame them at all, but at the time – at fourteen years old – I felt like I'd lost both my parents, and I was acutely lonely, often crying myself to sleep at night.

Michelle and I had started going out before Mum left. She agreed to it on the condition I chucked Sharon Chandler – another girl I'd been seeing. I liked Sharon and spent a lot of chaste evenings in her bedroom, listening to the Bee Gees. But I always had my eye on Michelle and Sharon's ankle-swinger cords were a potential problem when it came to Gary and his mates – I knew they'd take the piss. Being immature and embracing the shallow side of my personality, I agreed to Michelle's request. We'd snog in the porch of her parents' house, while inside, her sisters (Susan and Cathy) and her parents (Sylvie and Roy) sang in harmonies incessantly. It was like being with the Nolans, if I'm honest. I think the singing drove Roy a bit mad because once or twice I saw him sneak off alone into the back garden and rip up old cardboard boxes with gusto. But Michelle and her family offered what I was missing – a home full of love.

Despite my sweet romance with Michelle, I was beginning to turn from strait-laced, well-behaved David, to someone more rebellious. This rebellion was largely down to Gary Baker. Six foot three and trouble personified.

I was now leading a double life. One of these lives was spent with Adam in his bedroom, playing music, recording it on cassettes so we could learn the lyrics, then entering talent competitions. The other life was dominated by Gary Baker, his mum, dad and their intimidating, glamorous friends. It was a "thanks very much, Dad, for not standing up for me". It was a "fuck you" to my mum who'd abandoned me. I figured no one cared what I did, so I may as well do what I wanted.

Looking back, I can see that my sadness was manifesting as anger and rebellion. In order to self-soothe, I set about replacing my family with other people's. There was Michelle and the Von Trapp vibe, then Adam and his lovely parents Annette and Eric, who represented safety and kindness. Then finally, The Baker lot – loud and irresistible.

Me, Gary and his brother Grant bought booze at the shops and drank it outside on the council estate "The Circle" where they lived. I was out all the time but got a Saturday job cleaning with Gary when I was fifteen. A lot of the money we earned went on paying adults to buy alcohol for us, but with my first pay packet I bought myself an orange Hawaiian shirt. There was power in independence, even if deep down it was hollow.

Eventually, Gary and I found our own local –

The Skinners Arms in Hackbridge. Here we forged a community, yet another family. I was growing increasingly distant from my dad – Dixie had taken over and I hadn't seen or heard from Mum for months. Impressionable and desperate to belong, I drank with the regulars in the Skinners: Sue and John, Jan and John – strangers who became surrogate aunties and uncles.

Finally, Mum got in touch by letter. She and her new bloke John had been living in a rented flat above Sainsbury's in Purley, but they'd now bought a one-bed flat in Croydon. Despite the long absence, and the residual hurt, I went to see them. John, I found, was a lovely bloke and he doted on my mother. That was something. I was happy for her, and I compartmentalised my feelings, locking the angry, wounded part of myself in a box and creating a new one labelled "forgiveness". It was easier for me to deal with this new version of my mother than it was to confront the darkness surrounding her abandonment. In turn, Mum overcompensated by showing affection for the first time ever. But it was too little, too late.

**

As I've said, while it's perfectly possible to have had a loving childhood and still develop an addiction, it often stems from child abuse of some kind. But many addicts dismiss childhood emotional neglect as a valid source of trauma because it was unintentional. They weren't victims of open hostility or violence, therefore often don't realise they were subject to abuse. The fact is, a series of seemingly harmless but accumulative acts of physical or emotional abuse during our formative years can do a lot of lasting damage. Though none of us can go back in time and change the past, we can attempt to dismantle any false narratives we've created about who we are and what we are worth. Even if your parents didn't take your emotions seriously, it doesn't mean you can't. In fact, you owe it to yourself to give them the consideration they truly deserve – it's never too late for that.

There are various manifestations of what neglect does to our developing brains, and the most common include:

- PTSD (post-traumatic stress disorder)
- Depression
- Eating disorders
- Avoidance of intimacy
- Low self-esteem
- Acute loneliness
- Anger and aggression
- Difficulty trusting others

I recognise some of the above, and with sobriety, I can see patterns. Sometimes a single event at a critical time in your life sets a blueprint. My mum suddenly leaving me when I was fourteen haunted me for decades. In my mind, if my mum didn't love me enough to stay and look after me, then why would anyone else? And if my remaining parent chose a stranger over his kid, what was I worth to anyone else?

People talk about closure, where you finally get the answers you need from the people who hurt you, but that's not always possible. What is possible, though – and crucial – is that we try to understand that other people's behaviour (our parents' included) isn't personal. Humans make mistakes and we can all only operate with the tools we are given at an early age. My mum was ignored and neglected by her own parents, which led to history repeating. My dad was raised to feel that his value lay in superficial traits: his good looks and ability to entertain. He didn't know what else he had to offer or that anything else was required.

Rationalising things you had no control over is a critical part of the healing process – it enables you to forgive yourself and others. Over the past few years, I've talked to many people who've been affected by alcohol dependence, and a common trait is the self-loathing or negative self-talk it generates. Either they drank and hated themselves for it, one of their parents drank and they internalised it or their emotional needs weren't met during childhood – and rather than viewing this objectively as human error, they assumed it was because they were not worthy of love and/or did not deserve it. All of these circumstances can plant the toxic seed of low self-esteem and we start to treat ourselves without the respect we deserve. Often this leads to reckless or rebellious behaviour – we turn to drink, drugs, shopping, sex, whatever it is, as a form of socially acceptable self-harm. But the more reliant we become on these escape tactics, the further into the abyss we fall and, once again, history starts to repeat.

So how do we break the cycle? For me, the key thing has been exploring and understanding my past, which in turn led me to connect with the child I once was. At the risk of sending you running for the hills, I urge you to start looking after and listening to your inner child – because they're still here, they're still a part of you. I know this may seem like alien territory to some readers – it was for me, too – so I have included some suggestions below about how to approach it. In the first instance, I would always recommend seeking the help of a trained professional, as this can be deep, emotional work. You can access support via your GP. In the meantime, you could also try:

- Talking to someone you really trust. It may be your partner, a family member or trusted friend.
- Writing about your childhood in a journal. Find a quiet spot where you won't be interrupted, cast your mind back and start writing. You may be surprised at what comes out.
- CBT (cognitive behavioural therapy) is a brilliant way of recognising and changing ingrained

thought patterns and habit loops. There are lots of free resources online.

- Track down podcasts, radio shows or online forums that discuss some of the issues you may be tackling. There is so much support out there, you just need to spend a little bit of time finding your tribe.

As part of your sobriety journey, once you've made it through the potential physical withdrawal, exploring the source of your unhappiness, unpacking that metaphorical suitcase you've kept up in the attic and confronting past childhood trauma is a challenging but incredibly rewarding part of the process. You get to finally change the theme of your personal narrative – from unworthy to worthy – and start living the life you deserve. I do believe you need to get a few months of sobriety under your belt to do this, though. I call this the phase two of sobriety.

'Every child deserves to live a creative and meaningful life. Sadly, when alcohol is the family secret, children are more likely to experience difficult situations with family violence, neglect and other problems. Most parents don't choose this for their children; there are underlying problems they do not know how to deal with.

Our work is all about planning for a more positive future; an opportunity for children and young people to see that the world can be different from the one they've known, so they can break the cycle of addiction and go on to live happy and fulfilled lives.'

— Hilary Henriques MBE,
Co-Founder and CEO of NACOA

CHILDREN OF ALCOHOLICS

There are many theories around addiction. One is that we are born with a predetermined propensity for it – a sort of inherited addiction gene – that can be triggered by trauma. But through coaching some amazing clients in recovery, I know that as individuals we're far more complex than that. We're as unique and as magnificent as snowflakes. It ain't a one-size-fits-all scenario. Addiction can develop for a number of reasons, one of which is trauma, yes, but that doesn't necessarily mean it's lurking in our cells from birth, waiting for its time to shine – or rather, shit – all over us.

But here's a fact: children who grow up in families in which one or both of their parents abuse alcohol are statistically *more at risk* of developing an addiction and becoming problem drinkers themselves. They're also more likely to marry or have serious relationships with addicts.

Why? Great question.

Growing up with an alcoholic parent prompts 'maladaptive behaviour' in children. This means they can find it more difficult to adapt to life situations than kids from non-alcoholic families. Other characteristics can include finding it harder to trust others; feeling anxious and/or hyperactive; blaming themselves for the erratic behaviour of other people; catastrophic thinking (being hypervigilant to disaster and expecting to find it around every corner). Catastrophising often leads to an inability to apply rational thought to a scenario in which failure, harm or loss are possible outcomes as opposed to certainties. In layman's terms: always thinking the worst.

It's tough for these children. Life feels (and often is) much harder for them, especially when you factor in the additional feelings of low self-worth we explored in earlier chapters. Growing up with an emotionally inconsistent or volatile parent with weak boundaries, whose life revolves around self-medication instead of nurturing their child, creates a blueprint for what that child can expect from life. If subjected to a dysfunctional atmosphere during early development with a lack of emotional support, it makes logical sense for COAs to reach for the drink when they hit their own problems later in life. After all, they've witnessed their parents doing it for years – it's a learnt behaviour, it's familiar, it's home.

But don't forget – we're not all the same. Many COAs go to the other end of the spectrum, determined to break the addiction loop. Some are risk averse, don't drink at all and deliberately seek relationships with stable, nurturing people.

My wonderful friend, author Sarah Drage, is one such COA. She has written a really beautiful testimony of her experience for this book. Hers is just one story, but it will speak to many people who identify with the roller-coaster ride that is growing up with an alcohol dependent parent. Over to Sarah…

❦ My role in my relationship with my dad was the "hero" child. The responsibility I took on was to protect him. I was fiercely loyal to him. I did my utmost to control the situation, to try and save him, to do well at school and out of school, so that I could outwardly project this idyllic family life and demonstrate the perfect role model child. My theory was that if I turned out "okay" then people wouldn't discover our big "dirty family secret". My dad was an alcoholic.

My dad in his sober days was a fun, energetic and extroverted person. He was the life and soul of the party, he was "Stevie Boy", a successful businessman with a beautiful wife and three children. Life was idyllic for my dad. Until he lost everything through no fault of his own and, suddenly, we were catapulted into a life of poverty. A life on a council estate where my dad's mental health deteriorated quickly, and his drinking increased even quicker.

Money, as far as I was concerned, was the reason he was drinking excessively, it was the reason his moods were so unpredictable, it was the reason he was so unhappy, the reason we were unhappy. I desperately wanted to make him happy again. I longed for those days where my dad was "normal". The days when I would sit and cuddle up to him on the sofa, the days where I looked forward to him coming home from work. But when my dad was an alcoholic during my teens, I longed to not be around him. I loved him dearly, but he was draining, he was unpredictable, he was a burden.

My dad was my burden. You see, as much as I tried to fix him, I also resented him. I would daydream about having a "normal" dad and sometimes I even went as far as wishing him dead. I couldn't understand why my mum just couldn't leave him and why he "just" couldn't stop. I would always describe him in my teens as being not like other dads. You see, I didn't understand until adult life that my dad was an alcoholic. I mean, I knew he had his "quirky ways", but I just thought that was Dad. Yet ironically, I fitted into a category of a typical child of an alcoholic, I ticked all the textbook signs of being a COA. At the time, I just didn't know it.

There were times in my teens where I would challenge him about his drinking. I caught onto the pattern of his mood swings when I was around sixteen, piecing together that Dad's tone of voice would change, it was deeper and more aggressive, his eyes would be puffy, and he would have a red glaze to him when he'd had a drink. I remember challenging him one day. 'Dad, you're an alcoholic!' I screamed at him. I was never scared of my dad, in fact as much as I adored him and respected him, when he was in his "quirky" – aka drunk – moods, I would rebel and lash out at him. I hit him, threw things at him, and blamed him for the dysfunctionality of our family home life. He would just sit there and take it, but he categorically denied that he was an alcoholic. He was adamant that I was being dramatic and, if he really wanted to, he could stop. He justified it by telling me that he didn't smoke or go to the pubs and therefore he was allowed a "vice". He was allowed a drink to "relax". That was his enjoyment; but he was blinded by its toxicity, both literally and metaphorically, because it was our nemesis.

After a day or two of the silent treatment, he would jokingly ask, 'Have you calmed down now?' He would reassure me that I was being dramatic and that he didn't have a problem, and that was pretty much a vicious circle for the next ten years. Do you know what, though? I believed him every time, I trusted him, and I was in just as much denial as he was. Despite my logical brain tricking me into believing that he didn't have a real alcohol problem, my subconscious brain knew that he was addicted to it. But, looking back, I was so caught up in the stigma that I didn't want to accept it. I didn't believe he was an alcoholic because he didn't fit that stereotype. He wasn't homeless sleeping on a park bench drinking from a bottle in a brown paper bag. He just used to drink in the comfort of our home from the sofa at midday with the curtains drawn. He didn't struggle to walk or slur his words. He had mastered the act of disguise and was highly functioning. Outsiders would have had no idea. It was only us, his immediate family, who could recognise the subtle signs. I remember being able to identify whether he had been drinking from one sentence.

I got into the habit of texting my mum or calling her before deciding to come home. 'Is Dad in one of his moods?' I would ask. Or if he picked up the landline and even so much as uttered the word "hello" I would be making up my mind as to whether I was just going to stay out with my friends or go home and stay away in my bedroom. I just learnt to live with this. My days at school didn't consist of worrying about normal teenage stuff, like what was I going to do at the weekend, or what would I wear, it would consist of "please say that Dad won't be in a mood when I get home".

Family events or events in general were always interesting. I would make a point of asking my dad to just act "normal". I would ask him to speak normally. 'Don't use that stupid tone, Dad, please talk to people and get involved, don't wander off, don't leave after half an hour, don't drink! Please just act normal.'

Normal, normal, normal, what the f**k was normal? In my world it was sober, I just didn't know it at the time.

With that lack of understanding came a sense of isolation, loneliness and anxiety. I couldn't confide in anyone; I couldn't tell them because I didn't understand how to articulate it. What on earth was I going to say to people? I knew the connection with the alcohol but, as far as I was concerned, I was being "dramatic". I was terrified of telling someone because what if I was wrong? What if I would expose him to ridicule? What if social services got involved? What would people think of him? What would they think of us? I didn't want people thinking badly of my dad, he wasn't always like that. He was kind, compassionate, sensitive, loving, he was the life and soul of the party. He was Stevie Boy, he was my dad, he was my hero, and I loved him so fucking much.

I just wanted him to act "normal". So, I would do sneaky things to stop it. I would pour his alcohol down the sink, water it down, and mark the bottle to just check if he had been drinking. Blissfully unaware that one: he was physically dependent on alcohol and withdrawal could have been deadly for him, and two: he would just get more.

The years went by and, as soon as I could, I moved out of our family home. Not because I wanted to but because I needed to. I had to get away from that toxic environment, an environment I was embarrassed to bring my friends back to, and an environment where I constantly felt as though I was treading on eggshells. I wanted freedom. But I wanted to fix my dad even more.

I naively believed that money was the answer to our prayers and money would make him better again. It was that obsessive and naive ideology of becoming financially independent that consumed me, and I went on to choose a career based on finances and not my passion. You see, I used to love to sing and act, I attended musical theatre school when I was a young teen, and I longed to be on the stage. I was good at it, and I was passionate about it. But when I left home, I realised that it was not a "sensible" option, and that I needed to do something that would get me a well-paid job, something that I could use to help my dad. So, instead, I enrolled onto a university course where I studied Crime and Policing. I felt so proud to be able to tell people that I was going to university. I was the first person in my family to do so, I was defying the odds against me, the "council estate kid" was going to uni. Truth be told, I was happy because I felt it would make my dad proud, I thought it would fix him. I had dreams of being his saviour, his prodigy, his success. I was desperate to go against those stigmas we were tarred with. I was going to be the change, his hero child. I used to think that if I did well then it may be enough to fix him. I carry that constant approval and validation seeking with me still to this day.

Leaving home was my opportunity to escape those constant promises of "I will change" or "tomorrow, I will start tomorrow". I lived through thousands of tomorrows (literally). But leaving home wasn't an escape like I imagined it would be. It was a problem that was brushed under the carpet, something I was running away from, and something we were all in denial about. Also, I had lived with a person addicted to alcohol for so long that I developed certain unwanted traits that just stuck with me. For instance, I was overly sensible for my age, like regrettably sensible (if that even makes sense?). Wild nights out were not my scene, and coming across respectful was so important to me because I had been tarred with a certain stereotype that came from my postcode, and my "quirky" dad. I skipped the stage of impulsive irrational decisions. I saved my money, didn't get into debt, didn't date men that I wasn't serious about. I longed for stability, and I was always worried about making the wrong decision and something going wrong in my already unpredictable life. I was so preoccupied with seeking approval and validation that I carved out this idyllic perfect image of this young, respectful woman who had her shit together at nineteen.

However, low and behold, my third year in university I was twenty-two going on thirty, I was in a serious relationship with the man of my dreams and my now husband Reece, and I was pregnant, hiding my bump under baggy clothes and desperate to just graduate without anyone finding out. I was embarrassed. I was the child of an alcoholic who spent my teens growing up on a council estate, I didn't want to have the "young parent" stereotype attached to me as well. That didn't tie in with the image I was trying to portray. What would people think of me now? How on earth was I going to fix my dad with a baby on the way?

The irony was that I used to stigmatise my dad. I would call him selfish, weak and pathetic. I lacked respect for him at times. I cringe reading those words back. I was truly awful to him; I had no understanding or awareness that he was ill. I genuinely believed he was self-inflicting it all, that he could've just "snapped out of it". I was sucked into stigmas, and I was reflecting them towards my dad. I loved him so much and I just wanted a normal relationship with him. There were times my husband would hear me talk to him and he would shudder. 'How can you talk to your dad like that?' he would ask me. But he had no idea, I didn't even confide in my own fiancé Reece at the time, I was embarrassed. I was hiding our secret even from him. It actually wasn't until the very end of my dad's life that Reece (by then my husband) understood the severity of his illness. Reece was kind towards him, he was gentle with him, and he was patient. But Reece hadn't been let down thousands of times.

My pregnancy became a glimmer of hope in fixing my dad. When I eventually got round to telling him, he dropped to his knees and vowed to sort himself out. For the first time, he admitted that he needed to stop drinking. My baby was going to save my dad. Her due date was his birthday and became symbolic, it was his opportunity to be reborn. I remember crying to my dad when I told him I was pregnant, I was absolutely petrified, and in a state of panic. I told him, 'I've ruined my life!' He very calmly and beautifully told me that, 'You've not ruined your life, it's just about to begin.' From that moment, I wasn't scared anymore.

When my daughter Esme was born at 04.15am on Wednesday the 15th August, my dad was waiting outside the labour ward and came in as soon as he heard her cry. He had tears rolling down his cheeks, and I could see the unconditional love he had for her. But I also understood that feeling now, and so the bitter resentment towards him began. How could my dad put me through all of that? Did he not love us enough to stop? Were we not enough for him to stop drinking sooner?

I can't deny that my dad was a highly functioning alcoholic at this point. He drank mostly in the evenings, he was working, driving and even babysitting for me. He adored his granddaughter, she gave him back some purpose, and some light.

But slowly he began to get worse. His drinking soon got out of control and by this point there was no denying that he was 100% categorically addicted to alcohol. It was at this point in my life that I learnt to decompartmentalise the worry of my dad. I allocated myself certain times to worry about him, but it manifested elsewhere and I developed health anxiety, a severe phobia of becoming terminally ill. Years later, and after a lot of therapy, I learnt that the health anxiety was a manifestation of not being able to control my dad's drinking. It was a way for me to channel that sheer desperation to control the situation onto myself instead. I could control my own body; I could fix that.

Fast forward to the end of my dad's life and I experienced a sense of desperation and frustration like I have never felt in my life before. My anxiety was at its worst and I had no control over that or my dad. I was lost, and I felt isolated and alone, despite having a wonderful family support network. No one really knew the severity of my dad's alcohol use disorder and I was at a loss of what to do to try and help him. At this point, my mum and dad had separated. My mum was still amazing with him despite their separation, but as his eldest daughter, and alongside my two sisters, we felt a huge sense of responsibility to help him. We felt like roles had reversed and we were the parents.

"I forced him to get sober" – One pivotal thing that I have learnt is that you can't force someone to get sober, they have to want that for themselves.

Around sixteen months before he died, I knew he needed help. I felt as though I had to do something drastic for him to admit he was an alcoholic, not just admitting to an issue, but we needed him to commit to sobriety. His addiction peaked one day when he was due to go on a family holiday. He had taken annual leave, and he used it as an excuse to have a drink "to relax". I remember collecting him that day and he was in that much of a terrible state that ten minutes into the journey I turned around and took him home. He was volatile, he said some awful things to me, he was verbally aggressive, and it was impossible to have a conversation with him without him repeating himself all the time. It was at that point I put a stop to his codependency, so I called a family meeting and we all agreed that we would not see him or allow him to see his grandchildren until he asked for help. I checked in over the phone regularly, but I refused to engage in proper conversation and refused to see him face to face. It was the hardest three months of my life.

Until one day he rang me crying and he told me that he would do it. 'I will do anything you want me to do, I will give permission for you to talk to my doctor. Losing my girls is harder than what I went through, and I will do anything to have you all back in my life.'

Finally, I saw light at the end of the tunnel. I saw a change in him, and I was so proud of him. Exactly one week later, we had him booked into a community substance detox programme. At this point, he was physically dependent on alcohol and I had no idea just how bad it was. The doctor who assessed him looked me directly in the eye and told me that under no circumstances should we take away any alcohol from him until he started his detox programme. Yet, despite that, the severity of his situation still hadn't dawned on me. To cut a long story short, he got sober and we got our "normal" dad back. The dad I remembered as a small child. His tone of voice was gentle and calm, his face was more defined, his belly wasn't bloated, and the texture of his skin was back to normal with no red glaze. Dad was back! But with lack of understanding came ignorance and naivety, as far as we were concerned. He was no longer an "alcoholic", he was "cured". He did the detox programme and was thrown straight back into a reality that had changed so much after fifteen years of solid drinking. He had no psychological support and no community of peer support. Why? Because we were still in denial that it was that bad, and we were afraid to bring it up again.

Despite my dad discovering a life of sobriety, his mental health was deteriorating. He felt lost, confused, anxious, depressed, traumatised, and to make matters worse, his dad, my wonderful grandad, died in March 2017. It was then that I noticed a difference. Those "quirky" character traits reared their ugly head. My dad was relapsing, and I have never felt frustration like it. I just couldn't understand why he couldn't just stop, why he had to go back; why did he ruin everything? I said some horrendous things. I wished him dead, I called him a selfish c**t, I told him I hated him, and that it was his fault I was so anxious. I hated myself for saying all of that. I was angry and it came out in a nasty, ugly way that I regret terribly. He cried, I cried, I told him I didn't mean it, that I was scared, that I thought he was killing himself and I had zero control or ability to help him. He was literally killing himself in front of me and no one could help unless he asked for it. I can't articulate just how frustrating that was to watch. I cannot put it into words, it's just too hard. But, in an attempt to try and put it into context, imagine watching someone you love drown in front of you and you're unable to reach them, unable to pull them out of the water; all you can do is watch the inevitable happen in front of your very eyes.

Around a week before my dad died, I received a phone call from him. He was crying and talking about some health symptoms he was having. I quickly went to see him and he was curled up in bed shaking. He was bloated, and had a subtle yellow glow to him. I instantly told him I was calling an ambulance; I was convinced he had liver failure and needed to get to the hospital. But, in that moment, he took back control and suddenly he was the parent again. He was firm in his tone, he demanded that I respect his decision to stay home and recover on his own. 'I've done this to myself, and I will get out of this myself, I am not wasting doctors' time when there are other people who need help more than me.' He was adamant that he would not get into the ambulance and that I was to respect his decision. I answered him back with, 'Well I can't watch you do this to yourself,' and I walked away. I went shopping. I went fucking shopping whilst my dad lay at home dying from an excessive alcohol binge. But there was a part of me that felt dramatic, a part of me that felt as though I had got it wrong. Plus, we had been in situations like that hundreds of times, so I just believed he would be "fine". It took a lot of therapy for me to stop blaming myself for that day, a day that haunts me in flashbacks and nightmares. I walked away. What if I'd called the ambulance? Would he still be alive? Would I be writing this?

But, three days later, the inevitable was happening. One morning, on my way to work, I had a phone call from my sister. Before I picked up, my subconscious knew it was something bad. I can't explain it, but I just had this feeling that something bad was looming. My sister's tone was serious and direct. She told me to get to the hospital ASAP and that dad was in a bad way. When I got there, he was sitting upright in a wheelchair, his face was white, his skin was clammy, and he was cold. He was so cold. I cuddled him and felt a rush of relief. 'Thank God it's not that bad,' I uttered to myself. But he didn't recognise me, he looked straight through me, confused and dazed. He wasn't drunk, he was different, I had never seen him like that before. You see, his liver was not working properly, the toxins were building up in his blood stream, and his body was slowly shutting down. His liver had stopped working and, as a result, toxins and bodily fluids were accumulating in his organs. His lungs were crackling, bruises from where he fell over were getting bigger, and he was slowly turning yellow. Yet, despite all those symptoms, despite various doctors, surgeons and nurses telling me how seriously poorly he was, I didn't believe them. I was still in denial.

Eventually, he ended up in intensive care where he was placed on dialysis. He was deteriorating quickly, he was dying, but I still clung onto hope. I remember leaving the hospital to go home and thinking to myself "how dramatic am I being?" I genuinely thought I was exaggerating the severity of the situation in my mind, until the following day when we were called by the intensive care doctor looking after him. He took us aside into the family room to explain that they were going to put him onto a ventilator as the very last resort. He began listing everything wrong with him. I sat and stared and stopped him mid-sentence just as he was talking me through the stages of multiple organ failure. "Doctor, is my dad going to survive this?" He looked me directly in the eye and, with empathy and compassion oozing out of him, he told me that my dad had a 15% chance of surviving, that's if he didn't die when they put him onto life support. At that point, my entire body ached, my vision went blurry, my heart was pounding, and I was shaking uncontrollably. I walked out of the room and went to my dad. He was unconscious, his breathing laboured and his heart rate fluctuating. At that point, I begged him to fight, I pleaded with him to make it through. I was crying hysterically, and I felt as though I was about to pass out. Yet there was a part of me that felt selfish for asking him to survive. I knew how much he had suffered from alcohol use disorder, I knew how difficult he was finding it, how consumed by it he was. A part of me felt as though him dying would be kinder and that my suffering would be far less than his had he stayed alive. I couldn't stay around him much longer, and I left to be with my sister. Despite hearing how dire his situation was, I still clung onto hope. I clung to that 15% chance of survival, blissfully still in denial.

Just a couple of hours later, my husband, who had stayed at the hospital with my dad and took on the role of liaising with the medical team for my mum, sisters and me, came to see me and my sister to deliver the news. He held me tight as I fell to the floor in silence. All I could hear was my sister screaming in the background. He convinced me to be with him in his final moments, to hold his hand as they switched off the machine that was barely keeping him alive. I'm glad that I listened to him because one of the last things I'd said to him was that I hated him. I will be eternally grateful to my husband for talking me round to say goodbye, to tell him it wasn't his fault, to tell him that I was sorry, to tell him that he was the best dad and that he's the reason his girls are so fiercely independent and resilient. I reassured him that we didn't blame him, and that he was ill, and we just didn't understand it. We sat around him and comforted him, we switched off his machine and we held him tight in his final moments.

I was broken, numb, shocked, angry, bitter, guilty, and I was relieved. It was over. We could finally get on with our lives without stepping on eggshells. We didn't have to worry about him anymore, we didn't have to make excuses for him anymore. He was no longer suffering, he wasn't in pain, he wouldn't have known what was happening, and he was finally at peace. But my suffering had only just started. I knew from as soon as we switched him off that I was at a crossroads. I was already consumed with anxiety and my dad's death was my make-or-break moment. I just had to make sure I chose the right road. But I was so fucking angry. What followed his death was comments like "he only had himself to blame" and that "he did it to himself". I remember screaming inside and making comparisons against those who smoke and eat the wrong foods. 'How is it any different to a cancer induced by smoking?' I would clap back passive-aggressively. How dare they? I would vent to my husband. But he reminded me that I used to stigmatise my dad, I used to tell him to "snap out of it", that he was "weak" and "selfish". I said all of those things to him. I was also sucked into that mindset.

I'm told when you lose a loved one that it's normal

to feel guilty; "everyone feels guilty when they lose someone". Every time I heard that being said to me, I wanted to scream, 'You just don't understand.' You see, as far as I was concerned, I'd killed my dad. I saw him days before he died and didn't call an ambulance when I thought he had liver failure. I stigmatised him. The guilt was too overwhelming, I had no idea how I was going to get through that. I wanted to die. I felt a massive responsibility for what had happened. It was my fault. The day after he died, I booked an emergency doctor's appointment and begged him to give me something to help me "relax". I needed the physical pain to go away, I needed to sleep.

The cycles of varying emotions were too hard. I'm not undermining other deaths, but I believe that losing someone to a mental illness or an addiction brings about other complexities. I don't say that lightly either. There are so many questions like why? Why did they choose to do that? Did they not realise how selfish they were being? Or why didn't I take it more seriously? Why didn't I get him help sooner? Or why did I call him a selfish c**t? I think to articulate this the best way possible, I'm going to list all of the emotions that I felt after losing my dad to alcohol use disorder:

- Anger – I was angry at him for drinking, and I was angry at everyone who stigmatised him, including myself. I couldn't help but wonder whether he would have got help had he not been ashamed.

- Shame/humiliation – I was ashamed of him. Yes, that's a massive contradiction, but I was telling outside people that he had died from a heart attack. It was an easier and less awkward reaction.
- Bitterness – I was bitter against him for making me feel "dramatic" and bitter towards the people who caused his past traumas.
- Heartbreak – I was so broken, so sick, so terribly sad and hurt.
- Relief – I was relieved I didn't have to worry about him anymore and relieved that he was no longer suffering.
- Guilt – I felt guilty because I thought I had killed him. I irrationally believed that the police would come knocking at my door for not getting him to hospital sooner. I felt guilty that I had stigmatised him. I felt guilty for feeling relieved.
- Regret – I deeply regretted the nasty, vile things that I said to him out of frustration. I regretted not helping him more. I regretted being in denial for so long.
- Disloyalty – I felt disloyal towards him because I was having to divulge our family secret and tell our family what he had died from.

All I can say is that there was a minefield of emotion involved, and as much as it has got easier, those emotions still crop up from time to time. It was traumatic, depressing, and a lonely place to be. In fact, it is only recently that I have discovered a community just like me and my dad, where I have listened to and read accounts from fellow COAs and people addicted to alcohol. I'm learning different perspectives and I'm finding the answers to so many unanswered questions that I never got to ask my dad.

On the flip side to all this, his death has had some positives. Fortunately, I went down the right path when I was stuck on those crossroads. I decided to get therapy and stick at it, I decided to talk more openly and not care about the stigma, to have open and honest conversations, to embrace my identity and to be proud and empowered by it. He lit a fire in me that is burning bright, and he has inspired me to advocate against the stigma attached to mental illness and addiction. His experience has already helped people, and I am so determined to ensure that he is not just another statistic but a catalyst for positive change.

Which is why I now advocate so passionately. Perhaps it's the guilt that I have carried forward, or perhaps it's because I feel like I owe this to my dad. I couldn't do this when he was alive, but I do this in his memory. I still haven't figured all that out yet, but what I do know is that I speak so openly and honestly like I do to prevent others from feeling desperate, isolated and scared! I do this so that children of alcoholics coming home from school and disappearing in their bedroom to escape the bleak unpredictable atmosphere have some understanding that they are not alone, and so that COAs in general understand that it is not their fault, that they can't fix the issues, and that they are enough. We were/ are more than enough.

But I couldn't have started this journey without Soberdave. It is Dave who has wrapped me up in a community of kind, loving, compassionate and supportive people who understand exactly what we have been through. He has given me the confidence to speak so boldly and so publicly. Dave has answered the questions I never got to ask my dad; he has played a role on my dad's behalf. Without his guidance and without my dad's legacy, I wouldn't be telling this story today. I wouldn't be as empowered and liberated as I am now. Which is why I will be eternally grateful for the powerful work that Dave contributes to this wonderful community.

Sarah Drage

Watching a parent self-destruct, as much as it might create a blueprint for some children, is a cautionary tale to others. They grow up vowing never to become the parent they had themselves. It's complex, and what determines whether a child will recreate the behaviour and habits of a parent or not is down to many things: an innate ability and will, that complex set of wiring that makes us what we are. And, if at least one parent provides stability and emotional consistency, then that child's foundations are stronger. But though these children choose a "healthier" path, that doesn't mean they don't bear the scars of their experience and don't struggle in later life.

Being the child of an alcoholic is a different experience for everyone. NACOA (the National Association for Children of Alcoholics) describes thirteen different personality types of a child of an alcoholic:

- Over-achieving and perfectionist tendencies.
- Lacking self-esteem – feelings of worthlessness and inadequacy in certain situations and in relationships.
- Finding even constructive criticism hard to take.
- Intolerance of what they see as other people's bad behaviour.
- Fear of being left or abandoned – they might seek reassurance more than others.
- A tendency to either think the worst or create crises or catastrophes.

- Lack of nuanced thinking – a person or a situation is either "good" or "bad", there is often no in-between.
- Difficulty relaxing in social situations, particularly with people they don't know.
- Self-berating – blaming themselves excessively for failures, e.g., at work or in relationships.
- Being the "hero" – the one who will fix or save a parent who drinks.
- Panicking and finding it hard to cope with challenging situations.
- Fear of authority – positioning themselves as a child rather than as an adult when dealing with authority figures (e.g.: doctors, the government, employers, etc.).
- Withdrawing from difficult situations and being emotionally avoidant rather than facing up to them.

All of the above are associated with other conditions, including neurodiversity, so if you are worried about someone you know who exhibits any of these traits, talk to them, get to know them, and don't push a label of COA on them automatically. If you are an adult COA and you're struggling with life – perhaps finding relationships or work difficult, or often experiencing feelings of sadness, depression or anxiety – there is a lot of help and support available to you. Reach out to a friend, therapist or counsellor, or NACOA or Adfam for COAs.

Compassion is vital – whether it's self-compassion because you're a COA or compassion for someone else who is. COAs are dragging trauma around with them. They have not been properly equipped to manage their adult lives, given inconsistent care as children, or worse, they've been subject to abuse – emotional or physical. They might have been told to "shut up" or "be quiet" as kids, and grow up suffering in silence, internalising their pain, and keeping it at bay with a whole range of addictive behaviours, not just alcohol.

Because the effects of addiction go hand in hand with emotional and domestic chaos, it makes sense that a COA will cling to whatever control they do have, in order to feel stable amidst the turbulence. For an adult COA, this need to control can manifest both positively and negatively in society's eyes. From always having to be the best at everything (golden child), to controlling everything you eat or drink, or obsessively going to the gym. Control offers a kind of stability that is often not sustainable.

***

As a parent who drank, this area of addiction has been on my mind ever since I began my rediscovery. And, if I'm honest, it's something I find really difficult to face up to. I have a great relationship with my son and I'm proud to be his dad. He's grown into a smart, self-sufficient man. He's creative, kind and, I hope, happy in life.

The truth is I'm not ready to have that discussion with him, not yet. I want to when the time is right. But there's a part of me that doesn't want to force the conversation on him or inadvertently open up a terrifying can of worms. He seems happy and stable now, but if that changes and he wants to talk to me about my drinking, then I'll be here for him.

When my son was very young, I felt a strong sense of responsibility not to drink around him. As he got older – seven or eight, say – and didn't need watching 24/7, I wasn't always so careful. After his mum and I split up, he would spend part of the time with me, staying over in my one-bed flat. Once he was safely tucked up in my bed, I'd settle down on the sofa for the night and drink till I fell asleep. Anything could have happened while I was out for the count in a drunken stupor, and I wouldn't have been equipped to deal with it. Even now I'm haunted by that – wondering if my little boy ever woke up after a bad dream and came to find me for comfort but couldn't wake me up.

The older my son got, the less cautious I was. I have always had a good relationship with him, for which I'm truly thankful, but I still wince at some of my behaviour as he approached adulthood. He's never mentioned it, so there's a chance he didn't notice, but I think the likelihood is he chose to overlook it.

Our father-son evenings continued into his twenties.

One of our things was film nights. I'd cook him his favourite dinner – mixed grill – and I remember insisting that he go and settle down in the living room while I did the cooking. The real reason I wanted to be alone in the kitchen was so I could neck as many cans of Stella as I could before the meal was ready. After that, I'd have a modest glass of wine while we ate. At the time, I was so deep into my addiction, it didn't occur to me that he'd notice that I'd been getting tanked up in the other room. Thinking back to it, I feel ashamed for disrespecting him and his intelligence. There was one particular night I recall, when the effects of the kitchen pre-loading started to wear off once we'd finished eating, and the craving for more booze kicked in, I went to fetch myself a "pint glass of water" (aka half a bottle of vodka and some tonic) and sat back down, feeling pretty pleased with my stealth ingenuity.

Any child of an alcoholic will tell you they become like a bloodhound when it comes to their parents and booze. They not only start to recognise the signs – the glassy eyes, altered speech patterns, overbearing or extrovert behaviour, morose moodiness, aggression or self-pity (etc., etc.!) – but they can smell the booze a mile off. The parent may be oblivious to this acute antenna, they've probably convinced themselves they've covered their tracks well, but they haven't. It's pathetic really. It's also a vicious circle – the parent tries to drink the guilt away in an attempt to avoid facing the truth, trapped in a circle of destruction. I know this because I did it.

To add insult to injury, I unwittingly tried to draw my son into my cult. I remember buying him a pint on his sixteenth birthday to celebrate and saying, 'Here you go. You're a man now.' I've even got a photo of that day. He looks so young, so innocent, that I cringe at my actions – and the accompanying subliminal message about the meaning of masculinity. I hate to think I pressed booze on him and made him feel the way I feel now when someone tries to pressure me into drinking.

It's only once you start living sober that the reality of how you were as a parent hits you. It's one of the worst feelings in the world. The guilt, the shame, the self-loathing many adults feel as they confront their past parental behaviour is a perfect example of one of those walls we hit in sobriety.

***

So, what paths towards recovery can adult COAs take? There is no one-size-fits-all strategy and what works for one COA may not work for another. Depending on how a COA has been affected, recovering from the events of childhood can come from intensive therapy where you are encouraged to connect the past to the present. It helps you see how early negative messaging has had an impact on your decisions later in life, and sheds light on the way you see yourself and the way you respond to those around you. Self-compassion will form a large part of this therapy. For many COAs, learning to love and take care of themselves is a key component of overcoming what can be a debilitating lack of self-esteem and confidence. Understanding that you were not adequately cared for or properly equipped for adult life means you are not to blame for your choice of coping mechanisms. But wanting a more stable and contented life, where goals can be achieved, means learning to cope in a different way – a way that allows you to genuinely connect with people and create intimacy in relationships, rather than being terrified of it.

There are also support groups such as Al-Anon or ACA (Adult Children of Alcoholics) where space is provided in a group setting for you to talk freely about how alcohol has had an impact on your life. Meeting other COAs and hearing their stories will make you realise you're not alone, you're not a freak and that lots of people want to hear what you have to say. Since shame is a big part of an adult COA's mindset, knowing that your experience is shared by others can alleviate this and replace isolation and stigma with camaraderie and validation. Then there is the excellent NACOA, an online UK organisation and support group dedicated to helping anyone affected by parental drinking, and with whom I've done a lot of work in my role as a recovery coach. I was extremely fortunate to grow up in an environment where my parents didn't drink to excess (as I've recounted – my own drinking derived from a traumatic experience in my early teens), but the more I interact with these incredible support groups, the more aware I become of the all-encompassing destructive nature of drinking.

Finding a community for a COA can be transformative in helping with coping mechanisms, but also – and very importantly – in giving them that much needed sense of belonging, so often absent in a COA's life. A child who suffers their parent's addiction so often battles acute loneliness and instability from living in a fractured family, and finding their own community as an adult is giving them back a family.

Building resilience for all of us is an ongoing process, and very few people get through life without coming across challenges or trauma. But children of alcoholics can experience devastation from a young age and will learn quickly about the power of resilience. For some, who do work on themselves, this means they can actually thrive in the face of adversity, develop excellent communication skills and have a huge capacity for self-sufficiency, compassion and gratitude for what they have. The path for a COA into adulthood can go in many directions and it is not inevitable that their lives will be sad, unfulfilling or tragic. Using their experience, seizing opportunity for growth and dreaming big means that they can not only have happy lives, but they can shine.

'Never underestimate the power you have to take your life in a new direction.'

— Germany Kent

THE GENDER DIVIDE

This is a big one. Alcohol consumption and its effects, including health and societal attitudes, is even now a different ball game for men and women. You might think an alcoholic of any gender is just that, plain and simple. But not quite. And the jury's out on who comes off worse when it comes to this addiction. True, you tend to see fewer women than men hanging out outside Sainsbury's with that look in their eyes, stinking both of booze and bodily fluids. And when you think of those people in the pub, shouting and ranting incoherently, it's probably a bloke you've got in mind. You might then conclude that women don't tend to "sink that low", they're more disciplined, they have more respect for themselves. When women are drunk, they may be a bit lairy, but they're not violent, they wear clean clothes, they look better. They've just got a better handle on it than men. It's not as "bad" for women.

While there *is* an element of truth in this, the way women with alcohol dependency drink, and appear to drink, has more to do with the box society has long put them in rather than self-respect, discipline and control. Men are indulged when it comes to all addictions (and let's face it, behaviour in general) way more than women. Some psychologists or psychoanalysts believe that men are infantilised – they're kept as little boys for longer – while women are expected to grow up quicker and adopt responsible behaviour at an earlier age. And it is a truth that bad behaviour is still considered a marker of masculinity. Think of those movie stars who are idolised as "bad boys". Drugs and alcohol are glamourised for men but considered more shameful when they're consumed to excess by the opposite sex.

It's not fair, it's the patriarchy, and when it comes to recognising a problem with and being treated for alcohol abuse, the often covert nature of female drinking, the stigma attached to being a woman, a mother, a wife who has "drinks", means that women can remain undercover (or in denial of their habit) for longer. And their physiology – their anatomical and biological make up – means that long-term addiction to alcohol often takes a greater toll on their health and relationships, as well as their professional lives.

So, what about women and alcohol?

According to the Institute of Alcohol Studies, over the past few decades, women have caught up with men in terms of how much they drink, and it is women of between fifty-five and sixty-five who now make up much of that gap closure between the sexes. And when it comes to socio-economic groups, women from managerial "high-flying" backgrounds were found to drink more on average than routine or manual workers, and the employed drink more than the unemployed. Makes sense, as they have more disposable income. What's more, the number of alcohol-related female admissions to A&E services has been rising. There is also a lot of evidence to suggest that female health is more affected from lower consumption of alcohol than men, and that alcohol-related injury, illness or conditions are more common in women than men, including:

- Alcohol dependence: higher concentrations in the blood of ethanol mean women are more predisposed to addiction.
- Mental health: greater links have been made between heavy drinking in women and psychological disorders such as depression, post-traumatic stress disorder (PTSD), suicide and suicidal thoughts, and eating disorders.
- Fertility and reproduction: though heavy drinking affects both sexes, when it comes to fertility issues, it has a greater impact on female reproduction, including issues with conceiving. While pregnant, there is risk to the unborn child, including miscarriage and foetal alcohol spectrum disorders.
- Breast cancer: there is evidence to suggest that alcohol is a risk factor for developing this cancer.
- Drinking in middle age: older women have less

lean muscle mass, which fends off many effects of booze, and this tissue further deteriorates with age. Female liver enzymes, which help process alcohol, are less effective as they get older, and their central nervous systems become more sensitive. Put simply, they have the worst hangovers, some of which never go away.

- Studies have indicated that female alcohol abuse leads to a greater chance of mental illness, and because their blood-alcohol levels remain high after drinking, there is a greater chance of negative effects on the brain and impact on its neurotransmitters, which are responsible for mood and impulses such as suicidal thoughts.
- And when it comes to female fertility, even moderate drinking affects ovarian and hormonal function and can trigger early menopause.

Since the seventies in the UK, changing drinking culture has had an impact on women's relationships with alcohol. Whereas up until then a lot of drinking took place in the local pub, a traditionally male-dominated space, and beer or spirits were pretty much the only options (and again "men's drinks"), the advent of cheaper wine sold in family shopping outlets like supermarkets meant that picking up a bottle to drink at home was more accessible and acceptable for women.

In Grey Area Drinking, I talk about how drinking as a coping mechanism for women can be triggered by stress, professional or personal challenges, and traumatic lifestyle changes (such as motherhood and even illness). The pressure to juggle so many commitments can be harder on women, and though men also take refuge in the bottle through tough times, they are allowed to drink in a way that women aren't. Covert or secret drinking then might become a way of life. A glass of wine after putting the kids to bed might turn into two, and then half a bottle. And let's not underestimate boredom as a trigger for alcohol use. The niggling shame that women may feel while becoming increasingly reliant on that glass of wine or large gin and tonic creates a vicious circle. More is drunk to stop feeling bad, etc.

I mentioned at the start of this chapter that we tend to see more overtly alcoholic men than women in public, but there does come a point when alcohol dependency becomes severe, when stigma is replaced by a lack of inhibition and self-care in women. Subconsciously or not, we judge these women more harshly than their male counterparts. An intoxicated, unfiltered and aggressive woman is somehow more appalling.

SO, WHAT ABOUT MEN?

I don't want to over-generalise here, but it's true to say that many men are wired from birth to indulge in riskier, more dangerous behaviour. Free of the shackles of decorum and being "sensible" – traits that are, even unwittingly, unfairly forced on girls and women – men can push bad behaviour further and faster with fewer social consequences. And, in some cases, even grown adult men who are highly visible in public life can self-destruct and still earn admiration. Take George Best, the iconic seventies footballer. Though, in later years, his battle with alcohol dependence was not only transparent but documented, including "last-chance" surgical intervention, he repeatedly fell off the wagon. But by the time he died with his liver decimated, though his drinking wasn't applauded, he still retained "footballing hero" status amongst a certain generation. George's life was undoubtedly riddled with poor mental health, but his coping mechanism was somehow indulged because it went hand-in-hand with his talent and his playboy status, living life on the edge, the archetypal bad boy. The same could be said of the actor Oliver Reed, whose womanising was legendary, and his drinking highly destructive, and yet both things were so much a part of his image that filmmakers prised them in when it came to the parts he was given, right to the end, with his final appearance in the film *Gladiator*. You could argue that both George Best and Oliver Reed were exploited by the public and an industry that was invested in their wild antics, and their alcoholism.

As I write this, the actor Johnny Depp has just won

a domestic abuse libel case against his ex-wife, which as the trial progressed earned him even more devoted fans, who mostly saw a sensitive and troubled hero, and not an addict. I wasn't there, so I don't know the truth of the situation between them, and justice in his case may well have been served, but it's hard to imagine that if he was a woman he would be indulged in the same way.

That's not to say that men get an easy ride. In fact, the very pressure to be the bad boy, the life and soul of the party, or even tormented and interesting, is as hard as the pressure to be accountable and responsible and feminine that women experience.

***

At the beginning of my adult drinking life – back in the eighties, an era before widespread use of mobile phones, and, apart from some now classic video games, technology in general – like the decades before it, filling time for young men was more limited – sport, watching it on telly or playing football or cricket, gigs, the odd comedy club... and, notably, the local pub, where blokes of all ages dominated. In my local, men who'd been drinking there for most of their lives often had their own tankard kept behind the bar. If you were a regular, known to the bar staff, you only had to walk through the door for the barmaid or barman – "barperson" is probably the correct term – to start pulling your pint or preparing your whisky.

It was also a time when ordering a glass of wine was inadvisable, since most pub wine then tasted like paint stripper – but I digress! The point is, you didn't have to ask. The local pub, for many men, was a home from home. Welcoming, warm, non-judgemental... a place where they belonged, and a reprieve from marital issues, demanding kids, chores and worries in general. There was not much that couldn't be tempered by a Guinness or a few pints of their favourite beer in the company of other men like them. Maybe a game of darts, a spot of pool, or later in the evening, a tipsy attempt to offload incoherent emotions to whoever was behind the bar. Money worries, health concerns, fears about redundancy, relationship dilemmas or heartbreak... they were all put into perspective (aka pushed under the carpet) in those few hours down the local. At weekends, many men might have done a double-shift – pub at lunchtime, maybe after a match, and then again in the evening after tea, if there was nothing on the telly you fancied.

Women went to the pub too, of course, but not as much. In my opinion, women tend to be better at facing up to everyday challenges than men, or maybe they have an innately stronger sense of responsibility. It was just expected that if there were young kids at home, the woman would stay at home to look after them while the man went off to the local boozer for a couple of hours. Worse than that, many wives or girlfriends would then corral the kids into the car to go and pick up their other half, worse for wear and stinking of alcohol and fags, and bring him home.

The pub I went to was a typical Young's pub, and the kind of men I've just described were two-a-penny in there. One, we called him Charlie the Chippy, lived in the New Town with his wife Janet. The two of them had a kind of arrangement, all focused around Charlie's needs, not hers, where she waited at home while he went out, and then she came to pick him up when he was done. If she was lucky, he'd buy her a drink before they drove back home. Sounds like something out of the dark ages, but compared to the much more level playing field and improved gender equality of today, even the eighties and nineties were stuck in a retrograde sexist cave when it came to boozing.

When I first started drinking there, I had no real responsibilities and was generally out for as much as I could get for as little as I could give when it came to my drinking. My tipple of choice in those days for a while was a "light and lager", which consisted of a half a pint of lager, accompanied by a small bottle of light ale, both of which amounted to more than a pint. Importantly, this meant that over the course of an evening I would down six pints, rather than five. I was well and truly drawn into the patriarchal culture of boozing back then.

Drinking for me meant hanging out making superficial or jokey conversation with my mates until

I'd drunk so much I could barely speak. It created the illusion of being sociable, being normal, and importantly not properly acknowledging any feeling stronger than the need to use the gents at regular intervals. I was in a boys' club, and numbed enough that it didn't occur to me that I didn't really fit in. I wasn't a macho type, never had been. I'd somehow talked myself into another version of myself. Running from that sensitive little kid who hung around with my friend Adam playing innocent games – the type of kid who once upon a time would have been labelled "gay" by the laddier kids at school – into "one of them". My sense of belonging was so acute that being mates with Gary Baker and his cohort seemed like a viable option. Handed my first can of Fosters one evening at the circle on our estate in Carshalton, I was on my way. My role was a kind of court jester – getting pissed and being funny, entertaining them all with my inability to hold my drink – my party trick. I made them laugh and just about got away with my dread of aggression and violence. It meant I had to go along for the ride. One memorable coach journey on the way to see a rugby match springs to mind. It was packed to the rafters with drunk supporters around my age or a bit older, jeering and goading each other. I didn't join in, I sat there petrified instead. Then there was Cinatra's – the local nightclub. A shithole, the kind of place where you'd have to wipe your feet on the way out, but cheap drinks all night. We'd get there as soon as it opened and, in my case, often have no memory of leaving. I do remember waiting for cabs home at around four in the morning, still drunk, but not drunk enough maybe to avoid how miserable I felt. By the following evening, though, I was usually up for it again. Hair of the dog for me (and for many others) was essential for my survival. Being part of something – being the idiot who wanted to shine at something – even winning a bet that I could drink five pints of strong ale one after the other. To my friends, I was heroic, up for anything, and it gave me the high, the attention I craved. I barely thought about being abandoned by my mum. I had a special place in the world now. It was what I thought a man should be.

But to this day, bantering about football or discussing women like they are objects of pleasure and nothing else bores me senseless and doesn't sit well with me. I'm sure I wasn't the only one to put on a mask and pretend. It's a male survival technique that's still going strong.

***

Things started to change between the sexes and drinking culture in the nineties, with the advent of the "ladette". The likes of Sara Cox and Zoe Ball downing pints and getting publicly hammered while maintaining an aura of glamour and intelligence seemed to give the green light to women to play men at their own game when it came to living it large. Hedonistic clubs that centred around dance music as well as bountiful booze sprang up to rival the male-populated meat markets that nightclubs had been. Drinks like Smirnoff Ice, potent but nicely packaged in a bottle, were consumed instead of pints. The Spice Girls arrived along with "Girl Power" – chunky boots and miniskirts, loud, fierce and a million miles from demure. The message was female independence, vivacity and unashamed sexuality. Clodhopper boots and fishnets. Both young women and little girls were offered a new road to equality.

It sounds like a positive revolution. In reality, it was women aping the boys-club mentality. You had to have youth, a thick skin, a sturdy liver, be extrovert and energetic to keep up the ladette lifestyle. Drinking till you blacked out but going down laughing was and is still only really socially acceptable in women under thirty. If you're female and you try it at forty-five or fifty, you're something else entirely – a lush, a "state", sad and, to many people, disgusting. Another price to pay is exponentially worse hangovers.

Here are some characteristics of male drinkers:

- Boys usually start drinking alcohol at an earlier age than girls.
- Traits such as impulsive behaviour and thrill-seeking are stronger in boys and men.

- Men who suffer from anxiety or depression tend to misuse alcohol more than men who don't.

As with women, moderate to heavy alcohol use has an impact on male fertility, as well as sex and sexual performance. A reduction in sperm count, poor testosterone hormone release and impotence are all on the table for men.

There are societal and cultural differences in male drinking, too:

- White men are more likely to be alcohol dependent than black or Asian men.
- Poverty and life disadvantage affect both men and women when it comes to alcoholism and other addictions.

Though men are more likely to binge drink, they are also more likely to stay sober once they have made the decision to stop boozing. And, as I've mentioned, their biological make-up means that the effects of heavy drinking don't have an impact on them in the same way as they do women. This is partly to do with metabolism and the levels of "alcohol dehydrogenase" (ADH – the enzyme present in the stomach and liver that helps metabolise and process alcohol out of the system and into the bloodstream). Men have much higher levels of ADH than women, which means they absorb less alcohol (up to 30%) and have less blood alcohol concentrations. Men also have less body fat than women and retain less water (which helps alcohol distribute around the body) and will be visibly less drunk on the same amount of alcohol than women are.

In the long term, women don't have to drink to excess to suffer more severe long-term effects than men. They are more likely to incur severe liver damage, developing conditions such as acute liver failure, autoimmune hepatitis, fibrosis and cirrhosis. On the other hand, because they are more prone to liver cancer, men are more likely to die from chronic liver disease. Cheery stuff!

MEN AND WOMEN AND AUD (ALCOHOL USE DISORDER) TREATMENT

In general, women are more likely to go to the doctor when they're worried about their health, except when it comes to drinking. There are a number of possible reasons for this, including financial challenges (women earn less, or can be reliant on a partner for money). Other factors include:

- Women are more likely to feel they should sort out their dependency by themselves and not ask for help.
- They often consider alcohol abuse a psychological rather than a physical issue, hence they're more

likely to seek mental health therapy than treatment for alcoholism.
- The stigma, shame and embarrassment surrounding problem drinking is greater in women.

What's interesting is that my social media following is 85% women, and of the feedback and commentary I get about my work and on my posts, it's women who dominate. Men curtain-twitch – they might like a post and view a story – but few offer up their own experiences, or if they do, many are tentative, maybe detached, half in denial, half curious. This speaks to the masculine versus feminine wiring to a degree. That old trope about "coffee mornings" and bottomless brunches for the girls, where they put the world to rights and talk about their feelings, their relationships, their anxieties and fears. Then the men, who vent their feelings through the safe medium of sport or some kind of activity, where the focus is on "doing" and not talking. The truth is that the men who are most comfortable expressing feelings are the least likely to become addicts in general, and the ones who are emotionally constipated are the ones who numb feelings and run away from challenging emotions and old trauma.

But *curiosity* is a start. The anonymity of social media means that it is no longer as scary to face up to something you've been hiding, or that someone you love is going through or concerned about. The good news is that mental health in general has never been more recognised in society for its equal importance to physical health, and let's not forget that addiction of any kind stems from a psychological issue. Whether you are or identify as male or female, there is more help than ever for you, and you'll find some useful accounts and websites listed at the back of the book.

'Alcohol gives you the wings to fly and then takes away the sky.'

ALCOHOL GIVES
YOU WINGS

Or that's what it feels like when you're a few pints (or vodkas) down. Anxiety and sadness, depression and anger dissipate, and more comfortable, blurry emotions settle into place. You feel lighter than air, temporarily suspended above your problems. With alcohol coursing through your bloodstream, you can take on the world...

Drinking with friends rather than on your own is a socially acceptable pursuit. It softens life's hard edges and is commonly considered the perfect antidote to a bad day. For some, the habit is harmless, for others it's a dangerous gateway to a pattern of behaviour or routine dependence on a mood-altering drug. And perhaps the most dangerous time to get into this habit is when we're young because the arrogance and innocence of youth tricks us into thinking we're immortal. With our fresh faces and peak immune systems, it never occurs to us to think about the potential consequences.

Society is pretty indulgent of youth. Barring guns

and knife crime, drugs, obvious violent gang culture – you can get away with a lot. What's considered shameful in later life is merely a rite of passage in your twenties. Getting drunk in public, with all its messy consequence is "just kids messing about". Waking up with no memory of what you did the night before is funny rather than frightening. Go down the pub as a seventeen-year-old and ask for a lime and lemonade and you'll likely be labelled "the weirdo who doesn't drink" – because you're only young once, right? Youth is a time for experimentation, adventure and behaving badly. Who hasn't turned up for work in their twenties with a steaming hangover and a McDonald's breakfast and been met by banter-laced cheers from colleagues?

❛ ... I was born to drink I realise ... I never really had a choice, my family were huge partyers, the life and soul of the party. It was a very *frivolous* style of drinking, you know, it was never for commiserating, it was always a celebratory kind of drinking, so it was never something I considered *not* doing, at any point in my life. Well, until recently ...

I started very, very young ... stealing bottles of wine out of the garage, stealing beers, whatever I could get my hands on, and necking it at the rec down the road. I was always the instigator, always with the bottles of wine, the packets of fags. Growing up in the eighties and nineties, I was surrounded by alcohol most of the time, and my mum could whip up a glamorous party at the drop of a hat. It was all very romantic to me, and I never saw the dark side of it, I just wanted to join in ... I was passed out in a field in a cider coma for most of my teens. It made me feel confident with boys. I started to use alcohol then as a way of fitting in ... and I learned to deal with my emotions by pouring more and more alcohol down my neck ... *❜*

Victoria Vanstone – *One for the Road* podcast

Though studies indicate that drinking among eighteen-to twenty-five-year-olds is decreasing, it is still the case that those who do drink, drink a lot. They also drink more regularly – maybe enough to cause trouble, get lairy, black out or even engage in criminal behaviour. Depending on your peer group, the pressure to drink at a formative age can be dangerous. A lot of young people will "get it out of their system" prior to their thirties, at which point peer-pressure morphs to embrace professional achievement, family life and settling down. There is a greater sense of responsibility for both yourself and others.

But we are not all the same.

Whatever your sex, you'll have received subliminal messages about alcohol in the context of your gender. As a man, it's not just acceptable, but encouraged – a badge of honour, a symbol of masculinity. The expression "he can't take a drink" implies weakness or failure on some level. Similarly, if you're female, sipping a glass of wine is considered appropriate. It's ladylike, restrained. I explore the gender divide and alcohol in more detail in another chapter but wanted to mention it in the context of this one as I believe my gender played a big part in this part of my life. As a sensitive, emotional and damaged young man, I was taught not to show or talk about the way I felt. I truly believed the only option available to me was to drown my feelings in drink. And, when you're a young bloke, no one really bats an eyelid if you drink a lot. Drinking to forget was almost expected of me, so that is what I did.

CROSSING THE LINE ...

My transition from ordinary drinker to alcohol dependent didn't become obvious until my early thirties, though it took root in my late twenties. Before that, I'd been inconsistent in terms of booze consumption. There were periods of hardly any drinking – usually when I was in a relationship. But the in-between times, often marked by heartache, betrayal or loneliness were when I learnt to rely on alcohol to numb emotional pain.

At the end of my teens, my relationship with Michelle had reached the end of the road. She'd been a good influence – wholesome, close to her sisters and a fellow outsider who stood out at school because she studied hard and got good grades. With Michelle, I'd been able to easily express the affection I'd never had with my mum. Funny how you see obvious connections from a distance and come to realise that the right people arrive in your life at the right time. It doesn't take a rocket scientist to work out that Michelle stood in place of the mother I needed. We made it for five years before new horizons beckoned for me. Decades later, both of us laden down with experience and emotional baggage, Michelle and I reconnected. It didn't work out, but that's another story.

So here I was, knocking about with my mates, playing footie and discovering that alcohol was a pretty useful way of numbing any feelings of loss around Michelle, as well as a pretty good inhibition-inhibitor. Which came in handy when Gary announced he was going to fix me up with his mate Hannah. He described her as "a right sort" – an archaic and misogynistic term that would obviously now be cancelled. Despite the fact she was dating someone else – a guy called Kev – somehow Hannah liked me enough to dump him and we got close pretty quickly. It seemed like I'd barely finished with Michelle before I'd closed the gap with another woman.

With her high cheekbones, cat-like features and skintight jeans, Hannah was stunning: beautiful, a little bit dangerous, and a world away from Michelle's innocence. If I were to frame the contrast in terms of the original *Grease* movie, Michelle was the virginal, pre-makeover Sandy and Hannah was the spray-on PVC version, stubbing her fag out with a stiletto heel.

I was young. In my mind, I had outgrown the safety of my first girlfriend, whose upbringing had instilled in her the kind of old-fashioned values that meant she'd never look at another bloke let alone be unfaithful. Michelle made me feel so secure that I thought I was armour-plated enough to embark on a different kind of relationship. Or perhaps I was subconsciously uncomfortable with her loyalty, easy affection and stable family. Perhaps I was much more comfortable feeling unsafe because it was more familiar territory – as contradictory and ridiculous as that might sound.

Like Michelle, Hannah was clever and had a good job working in accounts at Sainsbury's, but the similarities ended there. Hannah's background was not exactly wholesome. Though her mum was a nice woman (looked a bit like Diane Coupland from *Bless This House)* and her stepdad "Bomber" was fairly straightlaced, Hannah's biological dad was a pretty unsavoury character. Tottenham's less innocent version of Del Boy Trotter, he was a well-known face who dabbled in dodgy documents and knockoff watches. Hannah's brother, Alan, a mini-me of his dad, was also a mate of Gary's and we got on okay despite an underlying hint of rivalry between us. We played football and had a laugh, but it was a superficial friendship. He stopped talking to me when Hannah and I broke up and I've not heard from or seen him since.

From the off, I had to get used to Hannah being lusted after by most other lads. As much as it got to me, perhaps it was part of the attraction. Maybe it was what made butterflies appear and nerves jangle. Things moved fast and we bought ourselves a maisonette in Tooting. Drinking didn't feature much at that time, bar the odd night out with Gary. We had a pretty regular, even cosy kind of setup. For a while. Deep down, though, I always felt she was out of my league, despite the fact she was seemingly keen and we got on really well. I was always subconsciously waiting for her to leave.

A couple called Graham and Wendy lived in the flat above us in Tooting. They were around our age and we grew to be a kind of foursome, hanging out together most nights. Our friendship was a handy distraction from the intensity of our own relationship, a relationship that in retrospect I don't think either of us were ready for. Graham and I were like a couple of big kids chuckling away to episodes of *Laurel and Hardy*, while Hannah and Wendy would gossip together. It was a bit like the scene in *Trainspotting* where the guys ask the girls what they're talking about and they say "shopping" in unison.

When Graham and Wendy moved away, the cracks in my relationship with Hannah suddenly became more visible. I also lost a job and with the mortgage to pay on the flat, we were struggling financially. Being a bloke in the eighties, I felt an extra pressure as "the man of the house".

Relief came when I got another job working as an engineer for British Telecom, and shortly after that we traded our flat for a big house in Maidstone: 48 Florence Road. Another diversion tactic to prevent us looking too closely at the cracks. I was still working in Sutton, so my daily commute was a 128-mile round trip, leaving me drained at the end of every day. Safe to say, it wasn't exactly conducive to a harmonious relationship, and I took my eye off the prize.

Here's where I've had to face up to some uncomfortable truths. I had this narrative for years that Hannah was the villain of the piece – the betrayer, the one who ruined our relationship. I told myself that I was the innocent bystander, snared by the local minx and then discarded when she grew bored of me.

But it wasn't quite like that.

There are always two sides to a story and, although Hannah had a substantial part to play, so did I. The notion of "working on your relationship every day" was new to me. I stopped paying attention to her. I thought a good relationship just ran on its own and if it floundered then it obviously wasn't that great in the first place. Which is like sitting by a log fire, watching the flames die, the wood turn to ashes, and then wondering why you're cold. It's lazy and mindless. But we were young and inexperienced, and neither of us knew how to fix the dynamic we'd unwittingly created.

My genius solution was to spend more time in Sutton, hanging out in the pub with mates. I stayed over some nights. I don't know how I justified it – probably that I was giving us both space, or that it was important to keep in contact with my friends. The reality was, I neglected her, and she must have felt lonely and unloved.

My sister was married to a bloke called Shaun at the time and we had some sporadic contact. When Shaun called one day and asked if he could pop round for coffee, I told him I wasn't going to be back till late and thought no more about it. I was clueless to what was going on. Clueless... and cocky. I was good-looking, still got attention from other women and Hannah and I hadn't had sex in a year. Feeling increasingly disconnected from her, my insecurities about being with her had subsided. Besides, I had a new partner in crime in Sutton: Dan, a male model. The two of us acted like single blokes out on the town, circling the bars and pubs, flirting with any female in the vicinity. Like driving a truck blindfolded at a brick wall, I didn't see what was ahead of me. I just kept on going with my blinkers firmly on.

Everything imploded, of course. Abandoned by me, Hannah had started sleeping with Shaun. Maybe others too – I still don't know. It's an understatement to say that it was a gut-punch when I found out. But I rode the moral high ground, moved out and told myself I'd known all along what she'd do.

My new place was a shithole. A crappy bedsit in Sutton that would've made Rigsby from *Rising Damp* recoil in disgust. A damp, nine-by-six box-room with a Baby Belling oven and mouldy bedding. Below me lived Andre. He had mental health issues and would shout at himself, night after night. I remember him throwing a chair out of his window once. It was grim and frightening. I had a good job at BT, which was lucky, considering the fact I was still paying the mortgage on the house in Maidstone, as well as the rent on the bedsit. But I was on call, which meant I could be summoned to work whenever and wherever. One night I was paged about a job, and on my way out I walked past Andre's door. It was open, a knife's blade sticking out of it. I thought I was hallucinating. Unfortunately, I wasn't. I found myself talking Sutton's version of Jack Nicholson from *The Shining* down from the ledge, somehow convincing Andre to calm down and come inside.

I don't think even I could fathom how far I'd fallen, from marriage to the fittest woman in town to living in squalor above a potential psychopath, my young life in tatters.

I had little contact with Hannah, despite the fact I was still paying for the house she inhabited – a house I no longer had keys to. There was a mix-up with a cheque I was owed from work, which resulted in me breaking in to retrieve it. Inside, stuck on the mirror in the lounge, were photos of Shaun, along with a message from Hannah in red lipstick: "You deserve the best, that's why you have me". I was nearly sick, but before I had the chance, Shaun pulled up outside. Despite it being my house, I hid in a bloody cupboard! I peeked out to see him arrive bizarrely dressed in basketball shorts, brogues and a shirt. The sight of him and everything he represented triggered what I retrospectively perceive to be temporary insanity. I leapt out and yelled obscenities in his face and before he could react, grabbed my cheque from the table. I ran outside and drove off. Not my finest hour. I'd reached rock bottom that day – unable to see the bigger picture or my role within it. I was too preoccupied with the injustice of it all.

I wish I could say I pulled myself together after that, but I didn't. Yes, I moved out of that shitty bedsit, but put on a long-running show of bravado I didn't feel. It was the start of a period of debauchery involving multiple women and fully integrating the concept of alcohol as an emotional anaesthetic into my life.

Hannah sold the house and, for various reasons, I ended up with a pittance as my share, just enough to rent a flat in Wallington, where I proceeded to behave like an Italian playboy: throwing wild parties, alternating between the four women I was casually sleeping with at the time, sunbathing naked in the back garden. Absolutely ridiculous behaviour. I felt I had to "go big" to cover up the mass of painful feelings inside; rejection, abandonment and self-loathing at how badly I'd fucked up. Where was the kid who'd been blissfully content with spending sweet, romantic evenings with Michelle and her nice wholesome family? I'd turned into a kind of Poundland Hugh Heffner, with some seriously dubious coping mechanisms.

I was around twenty-four and it was summertime. I was fit and Dan had become my unofficial personal stylist, so I was looking pretty good. I dressed to impress. I drank with colleagues as well as Dan, and one night a workmate from BT called Craig came out for a drink. We downed about eight pints of strong lager, ended up bladdered and crashed out at mine. It wasn't a one-off – there were loads of those nights, all merging together. Buoyed up by the incessant booze, staying out till three or four in the morning, I convinced myself I was just young, single and having a good time. I was over Hannah, and I was free, with several women on the go. I told myself it felt good.

I also deluded myself into believing I had discipline around drinking. At first, I never drank at home and definitely not on my own. I saved booze for the pub, where I'd let rip. A little later on, when I managed to buy myself a flat in Sutton and had befriended my next-door neighbour Andy, my habit moved closer to home. We'd go to a pub called The New Town or hit Diamond White cider in my front room. Sometimes I did this alone. But drinking without company brought up those dreaded feelings – depression, sadness, anxiety, guilt – which naturally I tried to alleviate with more booze.

Here I was, halfway through my twenties and coping with the failure of my relationship by ignoring it. My lifestyle could have been just a phase, something I'd grow out of, but it wasn't. I was a catastrophic combination of sensitive and hedonistic, with my suitcase of impossible things filling up in that metaphorical attic. It was the first of many of these periods in my life, and every time the stakes got higher…

HAVE YOU CROSSED THE LINE?

There's a saying: "You can turn a cucumber into a pickle, but you can't turn a pickle back into a cucumber." Once the cucumber begins the fermentation process, it crosses the line. The same goes for humans and alcohol. Once you've developed that resilience against the effects of alcohol, a couple of pints won't touch the sides, and in effect you still feel sober.

What you don't realise, or are too deluded to see, is that excessive and repeated drinking generally makes you a bit of an arse. And the sober people around you are beginning to clock it. Your life is only going to get narrower, until all it is is empty vodka bottles in the bin or a row of pint glasses on the bar, plus moments of extreme panic during fleeting moments of sobriety.

So where are you at in terms of the line? Are you still a social drinker who goes out occasionally with mates to celebrate or commiserate? Or are you a regular drinker? Someone who can't have a good time without it? Or who drinks to banish ever-present painful feelings? God knows it's an easy line to cross. In order to avoid crossing the line, you need to take action. Here's what I wish I'd known all those years ago:

- Be aware of your feelings. Notice feelings of sadness, anger or anxiety and try not to run away from them or push them away.
- The kinds of feelings you might experience when something traumatic or shocking happens in your life can seem unbearable, but they are your brain looking after you, building your growth and resilience – they are teaching you something. To put it in physical terms, if you burn yourself on a flame or on a hot kettle, the pain and the injury reminds you to take better care of yourself. If you start to think of your emotional responses as helpful, they become less challenging.
- Mood-altering substances like alcohol or drugs are short-term medication. When the effects wear off, the pain is still there, often more acutely than before.
- If you're sensitive and feel things deeply, don't be ashamed. You have a superpower if you're sensitive, and your highs will be glorious just as your lows can feel devastating.
- Express how you feel to someone you trust in a sober environment. This could be a mate, a therapist or within a reputable online forum. There is power in community support, and it may stop you reaching for the bottle.
- Many people find it helpful to keep a journal, charting their emotional landscape. Write things down or record yourself voice notes that you can replay.

- Go to an AA meeting. You can always sit at the back and say nothing, but listening to others share their own personal journey can be a real source of support.
- Listen to podcasts. Apparently, there's an amazing one out there called *One for the Road* by Soberdave. Never heard of him personally.
- Pluck up the courage to go to a sober event, there are lots of them scattered around the place now, including walks, activity clubs and sober socials.

Finally, and perhaps most crucially of all, there's a very good saying, which goes like this:

"The opposite of addiction is connection."

I couldn't agree more.

*'The inability to moderate is what
makes us alcoholics.'*

— Alicia Gilbert — founder of Soberish

GREY AREA DRINKING

What is "grey area drinking"? Well, it's the space between the extremes of rock bottom and every now and then drinking. Hard drinkers will either drink every day or most days – some of them all day, or they'll take a few days off in between binge-drinking sprees, when they really go for it. Modesty is not part of a hardened drinkers' vocabulary when it comes to booze. These drinkers are perhaps more easily identifiable as alcohol dependent.

Grey area drinkers may not drink every day, but they'll often have more "wet days" than dry. They'll also tell themselves they have a moderate habit and are not reliant on alcohol, but that's not true. Grey area drinkers may not be chronically hooked in the same way as hard drinkers, instead they experience a fluffier, softer version of the craving that hardcore addicts live with. There's also more of a reward mentality going on, which sounds like *"I deserve this"* as opposed to *"I have to have this"*. Although they may never become full-blown addicts, they are undoubtedly in danger of becoming addicted in some capacity.

GAD (grey area drinking) is an area I do a lot of work around with clients, and which affects a shocking number of the population –in the UK and globally. And it may or may not surprise you to know that women make up the majority of the GAD population. The reasons for this, in my view, speak to the gender divide when it comes to alcohol. There is such stigma attached to women when they are visibly big drinkers, it encourages many of them to either drink secretly or incorporate drinking into their everyday lives. They also tend to drink less, but habitually.

Research implies there is less "thinking" done around drinking by men. If they regularly exceed the RDAs (recommended daily allowances), they tend to do so in a more public environment. In my case, I drank both publicly and at home alone. But wherever I drank and whoever I drank with, I didn't do it in moderation unless there was a specific reason to (e.g.: hiding it at the start of a relationship). Unlike men, women tend to think more about who it will affect and how they will be perceived.

(... When I met my husband and I got pregnant very quickly ... it didn't even occur to me that after the pregnancy I would do anything other than have an odd glass of red wine and be sophisticated, you know, like just after I put my baby to bed. Within two weeks of my daughter being born, I was back on the booze. And again, I justified it. I was like, well of course I need a drink, being a new mum is stressful. I couldn't breastfeed, so I was grateful when they were like "give the baby some formula" because that meant I could still have a drink ... I had all of these rules around my drinking – like I didn't drink until my daughter had gone to bed, I didn't drink every day, I didn't drink *during* the day, I didn't drink spirits ... I thought that because I had all these rules that I was in control of my drinking. But actually, the rules were a sign that my drinking was in control of me ... *)*

Bryony Gordon – Writer and mental-health campaigner

WHAT DRIVES US TO GAD?

Grey area drinking often arises out of stress, anxiety or depression, or perhaps a challenging/painful life event that triggers the need for self-medication – something to take the edge off your feelings. But GAD is also a reliable source of social confidence and, for some, a helpful communication aid when it comes to difficult or fear-inducing situations, e.g. a breakup or a blind date. For lots of people, pre-loading is seemingly essential in such scenarios – the only way they can be themselves. Grey area drinkers come from all ages and stages of life; from teenagers to pensioners and everyone in between, they're a diverse collective, united by emotional avoidance.

Take the new mum who's dealing with a demanding baby or toddler – or both – whose life since motherhood consists of trying to nourish, entertain, pacify and clean up after her kids with no sleep or time for herself. She's lost touch with her old life – her job, hobbies, colleagues or friends without children – in short, she's lost her sense of self. She is tired, depleted, often lonely and increasingly she just wants to shut it all out for a while. On supermarket trips, a bottle of wine will go in the basket along with nappies and baby food. That glass of wine in the brief window when her kids are asleep becomes something she really looks forward to. It's just a glass of wine, she'll think, I'm entitled to it, not beholden. Take that wine away, though, and she'll be jumpy and irritable. In time, one glass won't be quite enough, and before she knows it, it's half a bottle. This is the point around which she's waking up feeling anxious and hungover (this is sometimes known as "hangxiety"), but probably doesn't connect it to her drinking habit, because in her mind she's nowhere near alcoholism territory. She doesn't actually get drunk and, besides, alcoholics stink of booze, have red faces, bad skin and drink whole bottles of vodka in one sitting. Well, she's not doing that! And she's seen the funny memes – wine or gin o'clock – everyone's doing it, it's not just her.

From 2020 and throughout most of 2021, during the dark days of the pandemic, it's no surprise that grey area drinking took off. It was an extraordinary, unprecedented time in all our lives, and undoubtedly caused shock and silent trauma. Lockdown during these years was, if not the same militant ordeal that it was in other countries, definitely a contributing factor in countless newly formed drinking habits amongst the population. The shock and trauma of a sinister new global virus, the ensuing and escalating restrictions on our freedom and a threat to lives not experienced since the Second World War turned many of us to drink.

Stuck at home during one of the hottest summers in recent years, boredom and anxiety converged and many of us took refuge and entertainment in alcohol. Not going into work meant extra stress and strain on family lives. For those with children, home-schooling on top of remote working was challenging, and a shock to the system. We'd never spent so much time with our families, and though there were obvious benefits to some, for others it left no distinction between work and home life, leaving little time and space to process the enormity of what we were going through.

If you were living in a small house or a flat with no outside space, it was suffocating and, as the weeks, months and years wore on, it became relentlessly claustrophobic. Add to that worries about money, jobs and a loss of meaning and purpose, many people struggled to find comfort in trusted sources, such as reading books or watching TV. To be honest, it was like living in a sci-fi novel, or a dystopian disaster movie. Except it was real.

Those without parental responsibilities, who were being paid not to work, took this unstructured existence pretty well – at least at first – while the sun was shining in the summer of 2020. As the restrictions eased, they spent days lying in the back garden or local park, either alone or bubble-bound, with a bottle of wine or a few beers on ice. It was like one long summer holiday, akin to being a carefree teenager again, drinking away the underlying fear and instability of it all. Daytime drinking was deemed an obvious, acceptable coping mechanism. People who hadn't drunk much for years, suddenly found themselves ramping up the units, and since it was a collective occurrence, any stigma or concern melted away, along with the ice in our Pimms.

In the context of my work, I heard tales of drinking vodka out of a coffee mug during a daytime Zoom call with the boss. It started as a one-off, but gradually became more regular. No one knew, so it was easy to get away with it. And the longer it went on, the more normal it seemed. Dependency formed. Without a commute, hangovers could be slept off. There were no colleagues around to see the subtle effects on your skin or the bloodshot whites of your eyes, or be privy to the smell of toxins leaking from pores. There was no reckoning – to other people, or ourselves. This heady mix of anxiety, instability and lack of censoring turned many of us into wayward children, living in the now and shutting out the future. It was like the pandemic had released our inner addicts.

As ever, I am the last one to stand in judgement. Given the existential crisis so many of us experienced, the collective explosion of grey area drinking was completely understandable, rational even.

Pandemics aside, drifting towards GAD is easily done. If you're in your twenties, and your social life revolves around drinking, dining, clubbing or gigging, and consuming alcohol is not only accepted but positively demanded, no one's going to bat an eyelid when you crack open a beer on a bland Tuesday. Or hit the fridge as soon as you're home and glug a glass of supermarket vino. Add to that the shitty job where you're still the office dogsbody and your boss is a nightmare, that large glass may evolve from "little reward" to "necessary coping mechanism".

In your thirties and forties, social drinking is still completely acceptable, only now you can afford more expensive, better quality wine and more of it. The kinds of stresses and strains you're subject to may have gone up a level or two: more responsibility at work, mortgages, marriage, kids, etc. Life is increasingly competitive and serious. As we settle down, we leave the more carefree days of youth and possibility behind. Dating and/or "playing the field" is replaced by routine and nest-building. And, as our significant relationships progress, romance fades and more practical issues take over. Working at relationships has to be juggled with financial and family responsibilities, and often falls by the wayside. Many of us sleepwalk into disconnection, then wake up one day and realise our other halves have become, if not strangers, then less known to us. The more emotionally alert of us will spot the signs, seek counselling or make time for date nights and reconnection. Others may simply experience a pervasive feeling that "something" is missing. They lose the ability to communicate effectively with their partners, express feelings or find happiness in things they once loved. This contributes to an increasing sense of discontent, which we try to drown as opposed to facing: drinks after work, a few beers or wines when you get home. We might tell ourselves we're just winding down and relaxing, but what we're actually doing is avoiding reality. If we don't work on sourcing or sharpening the emotional tools required to cope when our lives hit sticky patches and our stability is threatened, then we will flail when even low-grade shit hits the fan. Having a couple of drinks at the end of the day is not just welcome relief, it can easily become essential.

But still, you're not an alcoholic, are you? There's no park bench in the mix. it's fine.

Does any of this strike a chord? Perhaps you feel a bit uncomfortable reading it, or you recognise one of your friends or loved ones in one of the above examples? If that's the case, it's probably time to examine your/their alcohol consumption and weigh up what it's actually doing for you/them. I guarantee it is taking more than it's giving. Good quality sleep, healthy relationship and a clean bill of health are the first three that spring to mind. Alcohol, even small amounts of it, too often, is not your friend. End of.

Signs that you may be a grey area drinker:

- You find yourself feeling bad when you wake up sometimes. Even though you mostly function well – you go the gym, generally eat a healthy balanced diet, have a solid group of friends, a strong relationship with your life partner, etc. – there are too many days when you feel anxious, irritable or simply below par. You can't put your finger on why you feel this way, so you don't tell anyone, but the feelings lurk all the same.

- While you're certainly not a full-on out-of-control drinker, you can't completely take it or leave it either. Does the prospect of not drinking on a night out or a social event feel depressing, and like it won't be any fun? Does it make you panic, even if only slightly?

- You like to think you have discipline and make healthy choices – you've done Dry January, for example, and it was fine – but your achievement is tied up with competitiveness or social perception rather than good health. You want to *appear* as if you have willpower, that you're together, strong and in control. But take away the "challenge" and insert temptation – a breakup with your other half, a missed promotion, a birthday or a two-week holiday in the sun – and alcohol is right back on the menu.

- To other people, your drinking doesn't seem problematic: you're not a drunk, you're good company and you seem fun and happy. And you're keen for that impression to remain. If anyone were to ask you about it, you'd say you drink about as much as most people in your social circle, in fact you know people who drink way more than you do. Are you sounding a little defensive?

- Are you going into work with a hangover, however mild, more than once a week? Are you finding it hard to concentrate when you get there? Are you less tolerant? Snapping at your partner or kids in the mornings, maybe? Or colleagues at work.

Your grey area drinking may not be ruining your life, but it is surreptitiously stopping you from making the progress you want to in your life. And that niggly, uncomfortable feeling is your subconscious telling you that you're not firing on all cylinders. Alcohol impedes us. It does not give us wings. It stops us from experiencing our lives fully and reaching our full potential.

CRIKEY! HOW DO I NIP IT IN THE BUD?

- First of all, you have to make a firm decision to take a break. And by that, I mean a sustained period of no drinking at all. Giving yourself "reward" days, like weekends only, is not going to work, you're more likely to binge and your mindset is still tuned to booze being a reward after a period of abstinence.
- Start with thirty days. Make yourself accountable by telling loved ones, close friends and family that you're going to be sober for that period of time. Go public with it. This is CRUCIAL.
- Choose a mentor. A close friend, someone who'll support you through it (and beyond if you choose

sobriety for good). Someone you can enjoy non-drinking with. Trips to the cinema, coffee dates, walks, etc.

- Without putting too much pressure on yourself, revisit some hobbies, activities or sports you once enjoyed that don't involve alcohol. Art classes, baking, tennis, five-a-side footy, making a playlist on your phone – whatever!

- Change up your evening routine. If you associate certain things with having a beer or five/half a bottle of wine, then avoid them and do something else instead. Schedule a run after work or a trip to a bookshop or a gallery. Try something creative. Not to sound like your Great Aunt Mildred, but jigsaw puzzles are sometimes a lifesaver. They get your brain working and they're incredibly satisfying. And you're inadvertently ticking the "active mindfulness" box – because mindfulness doesn't have to be all candles and omming.

- Practise positive "ing"s, like running, walking, cooking, knitting, painting. Avoid the negative "ing"s: smoking, drug-taking (and drinking, obviously).

- Connect with a community of like-minded people. Groups online that motivate members to stay sober and share the experience. My Instagram @soberdave has an amazing community who'd welcome you with open arms. The reason Dry January is so effective is that it gives those with concerns about their drinking the opportunity to embark on a period of sobriety with solidarity instead of stigma. When I do my "Dryjansoberdave" the success rate is phenomenal because fundamentally we're pack animals. Feeling part of a community, feeling looked after and understood is not only incredibly motivating, it's part of our DNA.

- Make it non-negotiable. Make a formal pact with yourself and start every day with a sobriety mantra: "Today I will not drink". Empower yourself, recognise that you are in control.

- Make it a mission to eat well in order to strengthen your body and boost your immune system. Channel the energy you normally spend plotting your pints into creating a tasty and nutritious eating regime with plenty of greens, fruit, fibre, vitamins and antioxidants as possible. Avoid processed foods, sugars and excessive rich food. Eat regularly to keep your blood sugar levels balanced – it helps stabilise your mood and any cravings.

- Make sure you get plenty of sleep (eight hours a night if possible), including power naps if you feel like them. Your body needs to repair itself and recuperate as it sheds the toxins from accumulated drinking.

- Giving up such a pernicious habit as drinking is a feat on its own, so don't try and take on the world. Going on a strict diet or exercise regime in an effort to replace the high of drinking is going to be too much, and is essentially just replacing one kind of addiction with another. Be nice to yourself, and if you fancy a bit of chocolate every now and then, or a day lazing in bed, then do it. Dark chocolate is a great idea, higher in antioxidants and a little goes a long way.

- Invest in some vitamin D spray, which you can spritz under your tongue to help boost the immune system.
- Magnesium helps you to regulate your nervous system. Magnesium cream is great as the body sometimes finds it hard to process in tablet form.
- L-Glutamine helps reduce cravings.
- Milk Thistle is good for liver detoxification.
- Vitamin B1 or Thiamine is an essential nutrient that all tissues of the body need to function properly
- Taurine is good for calming down the nervous system.
- Omega 3 capsules can help to lower your blood pressure and aslo fight depression.

If you can learn to be in control of or eliminate the alcohol pattern you've got into, the results can be transformative. Here's the treasure trove you've got in store:

- No more "hangxiety".
- Better quality sleep.
- Increased fitness.

- Probable weight loss (if necessary).
- Reduction of internal fat around all major organs.
- More energy.
- A stronger immune system.
- Better mental and physical health.
- Better communication within close relationships and friendships.
- Increased capacity for true intimacy.
- Higher performance at work.
- More productive and fulfilling weekends.
- Better perspective and increased clarity around problems.
- Brighter eyes, a bushier tale, clearer skin and an infinitely nicer natural scent!

You have to fill your sober toolbox up with an array of different tools, and some days you use more than others, but when you combine them, mixed with positivity, connection and faith, you can truly start to distance yourself from the toxic relationship you have had with alcohol.

You CAN take control of your life and begin to live the life that you truly deserve because you are enough.

'Strength of mind rests in sobriety;
for this keeps your reason unclouded
by passion.'

— Pythagoras

CHOOSING SOBRIETY

For many people, choosing sobriety is a practical, rational "lifestyle" decision, rather than a positive act born of desperation. Let me clarify that a bit. Anyone with a demanding job, a young family or any other kind of external responsibility knows that even a couple of nights a week of drinking can take its toll. It wrecks sleep, affects performance at work and hinders our ability to engage properly with our kids. Waking up with a hangover as a toddler crawls all over you is not fun, and snapping at your partner because your head hurts can ruin the day for everyone.

These lucky (yes, lucky) people are usually not hardened alcoholics. Adversely, it's their intolerance for booze – even half a bottle of wine or a couple of pints – that works in their favour. They take a logical approach: why would I continue to do something that is spoiling my quality of life? It's not worth it, they decide. And although they might miss the pub and its social benefits or that glass of wine they have with dinner, they've weighed it up and the pros just don't outweigh the cons. For them, sobriety means feeling clear-headed, fully present and more energetic. As the weeks go by, alcohol makes a full exit from their lives without fanfare, and they know it's the best decision they've ever made. For these people, sobriety is an uncomplicated decision. I'm not saying it's easy – they'll have the odd craving for sure, but it's a world away from what a truly alcohol dependent person experiences at the prospect of never drinking again. For anyone to successfully eliminate a serious habit from their lives, they have to start with the question:

Am I prepared to do whatever it takes to change my life for the better?

If you can say yes with conviction, then you can do it. You can choose to be sober. Don't panic if you're not there yet! It will come. Our lives are a collection of infinite decisions, from the mundane – what are we going to have for breakfast? – all the way through to the life-changers – should I leave my job/partner/the country? The more profound the decision, the better it is to take it one step at a time. When it comes to alcohol, it's crucial to avoid projecting and panicking that you'll never hold out for a whole week, or a month or a year. Focus on the first day, then the next one, then the one after that. It's a cliche for a reason. But I'm getting ahead of myself (and probably you) here…

When I stopped drinking, it may have seemed like an instant decision in response to a specific question. But it wasn't. For a long time, I had felt it growing inside me – the weariness of it all, the knowledge that my time with alcohol had to come to an end. I was in my fifties, and I was sick to death of being sick to death of it all.

The year leading up to my decision to quit was 2018 and it was horrendous – a seemingly endless series of catastrophic events. My drinking was worse than ever, and my relationship was in trouble. My legendary weekend in Eastbourne took place at Easter, which was a low point to put it mildly. I can't say it helped that my doctor prescribed a double dosage of my antidepressants just before the trip. And, obviously, he didn't know how much I was drinking at the time – because he didn't ask!

The vast quantities of alcohol and strong meds proved a toxic cocktail. Not only was I off-my-head pissed for several days straight, I was verging on psychotic. When I got back, it was clear I had alcohol poisoning and my wife made me an appointment with a new doctor. I was with her for an hour, rather than the allotted eight minutes. All I remember is the all-consuming shame and self-loathing coursing through my body. I had an exam for my counselling course later that week, which I was completely ill-prepared for. Arriving at the examination centre, I realised to my horror that I had been allotted the trickiest "client" as part of the test, which I had to perform in front of two instructors. Needless to say, I failed.

Money was tight and we were getting a new extension built, so in desperation I sold my Rolex Batman for £10,000. The guy I sold it to claimed it never arrived, so I was forced to reimburse him. Now I had no money and no watch. I got the money back eventually, after months of stress and self-medication (of course). The whole ordeal cemented my belief that I was destined for failure at every turn.

That July, my mum had a lethal fall. She was found on her garden path, unable to move. It was the beginning of the end for her. Attempting to care for her while her dignity drained away was a profoundly emotional experience – raw and devastating. In hindsight, Mum's fall and the subsequent time we spent together through her final weeks gave me the jolt I needed. But back then, I was enmeshed in such extreme misery and guilt, I didn't realise.

It did give me the chance to say what I'd wanted to say to her all my life: that I loved her, she was the best mum I could have wished for, and that I forgave her. I don't think she understood but being able to express those feelings helped me. As a dysfunctional man of fifty-four by then, I knew firsthand how fallible and imperfect humans were. Perhaps I was showing Mum the same compassion I wanted to give myself but didn't know how.

As I held her hand tightly, I clicked my fingers in

front of her now bright turquoise eyes. She didn't even blink. Her breath was shallow but present. I told her I loved her again and then – silence. I knew instinctively that she was moving on to wherever it is we go, and I felt in my soul that she would be okay. Later that day, I got blind drunk.

* * *

Let's be honest. You're reading this book because you think or know you have a problem with alcohol and are contemplating doing something about it. Perhaps a good question to ask at this point is this one:

Why do we keep drinking when we think or even know it's time to stop?

SELF-IMPOSED NARRATIVES

When you're in the grip of alcohol, your sense of worth dwindles as you lurch from one drink to another. You lose sight of who you are, what you have to offer and what life has to offer you. You are probably a less than present parent or partner or both. You forget what you mean to other people, as well as to yourself. You forget that you are in charge of your own life and that you have the power to change it. When our self-belief stocks are low, it feels nigh on impossible to make big life changes. "I'll never be able to do it, so why bother?"

Sound familiar? You need to dig deep. If you don't believe you can effect a change within yourself, you won't. Rewriting this self-imposed narrative from "I can't" to "I can" or even "What if I could?" is vital in terms of habit change, but it can be challenging. Like anything worth doing, it does take time and effort, preferably with the help of a good therapist, coach or other support system. Or, failing that, a book like this one.

When I drank, I was always a "glass half empty" person (in more ways than one). I found hundreds of reasons to avoid change. But when I did finally take my blinkers off, I saw the world and my part in it completely differently. It was a bit like coming out of prison after years of being institutionalised, and realising you're free in a world that is bold and bright and beautiful. Albeit very different.

THE MYTH OF MODERATION

We've all said it: 'I'm cutting down.' But where does it actually get us? Can we ever really moderate? It depends on what type of drinker you really are. Social drinkers don't drink with the same goal as alcoholics. For them it is more of an accessory than a crutch. Take alcohol away and, yes, they might notice its absence, but they won't feel like a life raft has disappeared. Seeing it as something they want rather than need means they can stop when they've had one or two.

Dependent drinkers can't stop because they have to keep filling the void. Two glasses of wine won't touch the sides and they know it. For them, it is all or nothing. For me, I was like a greyhound out of the trap as soon as the first glass went down my gullet. It's easy to be in denial about this, but ask yourself now: is this me? Do I struggle to stop after one or two?

For some, they'll manage a week or two of abstinence and start romanticising the booze. They forget the hangovers, the self-loathing and shame, and focus on the "good times". And with that comes the fateful "just one won't hurt". It's akin to being with an abusive or coercive partner. You leave because you can't take any more pain, but within weeks, you get the rose-tinted glasses on and focus on how charming or sweet they could be. Maybe things will be different this time. You go back. You fall straight back into the trap. It's the same with alcohol.

The best thing you can do when attempting sobriety is to take moderation out of the equation altogether. Drinkers are generally all or nothing people, so use it to your advantage. Do you want all of the booze? How has that worked out for you so far? Or do you want none of it? 'I just want to be the kind of person who can have a couple at Christmas or a glass of champers at a wedding.' I hear you. But I'm guessing you've tried that. So, I ask you again, how has that worked out for you so far?

There is no halfway house. It's all or nothing. You have to decide. I get that it's scary – don't panic if you're still teetering towards the "all" side of things. Just keep reading with an open mind.

THE 'REWARD' MENTALITY

Another key component of moderation is the concept of "reward". You tell yourself you're only going to drink two days a week, so naturally you binge at the weekend. You spend the next two days sober, but realistically you're just recovering from the weekend. By Wednesday, the alcohol's finally left your system and you're feeling pretty good. You're smashing this no drinking malarkey! So, you decide to reward yourself with a midweek snifter. This mindset is never going to get you anywhere because you still see booze as the prize. But what are you actually giving yourself?

For a real chance at successful sobriety, you need to adjust your mindset and start seeing alcohol for what it actually is: enemy number one – something that does not serve you, never has and never will. Something you are choosing to leave behind for good. Getting real about why you've been hanging on to this enemy, this toxic friend, is part of the recovery process. So, I'm going to ask you right now. What does alcohol do for you? Why do you like it so much? Those aren't rhetorical questions – I want you to really think about them.

A COUPLE OF EXERCISES...

If you're still in two or even three minds about this whole sobriety thing, that's fine. That's normal. The following exercises are designed to help you evaluate your relationship with alcohol. It may shed some much-needed light. I'd recommend doing them in a dedicated journal or notebook (I'll talk about the value of journalling later on), but if all you've got to hand right now is a piece of paper, that'll do the trick. Just make sure you hang on to it. It will stand you in good stead later on.

- Make a list of all the reasons why you want to give up drinking.
- Make a list of all the reasons why you want to keep drinking.
- Which one is more compelling?
- Take some time to visualise a point in the future when you've conquered the booze, when you're completely happy to socialise without a drink in your hand. It may seem a mere pipe dream right now but believe me when I say it *is* possible. That day *will* come and, when it does, your life will be

vivid and full of potential. Just imagine for a second that you're there. Take some time to really visualise it. Where are you? Who are you with? What does it feel like to be you in this moment knowing that you are finally free?

Sobriety is a decision only you can make. Interventions by family and friends will add pressure, but they won't effect the change unless you truly want it. It's about recognising what you've got to lose, as well as what you have to gain by ousting this controlling, abusive substance from your life. And if you're sitting there thinking, "I'll wait for the right time", I'm here to tell you that there isn't one. There is always a reason to delay your first attempt. A wedding, birthday, holiday – Christmas, perhaps. But that's life. It doesn't just stop because you want to give up booze. We have a tendency to live with the earworm "I'll do it when..." so be honest with yourself about this. How many times have you used this notion of "finding the right time" to delay the inevitable? Recognise it for what it is: delaying tactics delivered directly from your chimp brain because it's terrified of change or failure or both.

Now is the time.

*'You cannot swim for new horizons
until you have courage to lose sight of the shore.'*

— William Faulkner

TAKING THE PLUNGE

We are all wired differently, so our goal-tackling methods will vary. There is no right or wrong way, there is simply our belief system, our values and our motivation. But whoever you are and however you tick, you need to make a personal plan of action. I'd recommend jotting some notes and ideas down as you read the rest of the chapter.

Some people, like Johnny Lawrence, for example, prepare for their breakup with booze like others might prepare to end a relationship. Going cold turkey wasn't going to work for Johnny and he knew he had to say goodbye properly. His method both acknowledged the significant role alcohol had played in his life, and the fact that it was over. He included his wife in his plans for the sake of transparency and support. This was a significant and brave act. Alcohol dependents are so often too caught up in shame and secrecy to seek help in this way, but by involving his wife, Johnny made a bold commitment – both to himself and to his relationship. When the time came, Johnny's wife left him alone to perform his final ritual. He finished the wine he had left and drank the last of his whisky. He told me that when the last drop had gone, he sat and cried until the early hours of the morning, as though grieving a lost love. He confronted his vulnerability head on.

Perhaps this idea appeals to you? Or perhaps you're more of a cold turkey fan? Perhaps you need the support of an online community who turn sobriety into a fun challenge based on positive psychology? Or perhaps you like the structured approach of the 12-Step programme within AA? Whatever method you think will work best for you, below are some useful tips applicable to everyone.

THE TOOLBOX

Whatever your route, you'll need an emotional and practical toolbox. It's a bit like going to B&Q – you grab a trolley, circuit the place and select all the tools you'll need for the job ahead. Your toolbox is tailor-made for you. Not everyone needs the same kit. It's important to take time to really examine who you are and identify the key obstacles or challenges ahead, as well as the elements of the process you'll find easiest to navigate. For me, meditation has never worked but breath work does. I hate running but I love a good walk. It's the same when broaching habit change.

If you need the in-person support of AA, make sure

you know when and where the meetings are, diarise and commit to them. If you prefer to do things online, try curating an Instagram feed of motivational accounts where like-minded people share their journeys. There is a wealth of online forums across all platforms, so do some research. It's a bit like going shopping – you have your own taste in clothing, so head to the shops that work for you.

WHAT TO EXPECT?

Hello Feelings!
You may find your feelings feel very close to the surface when you go sober. They might feel raw, sometimes hard to bear, but this is completely normal, and necessary. Feelings you've had packed away for a long time are coming back for a reason, so that you can face them head on, and taking one day at a time, confront their source and how to learn to live with them.

The Pink Cloud
There is a euphoria that comes in early sobriety known as the "pink cloud". It's a period of optimism, adrenaline and excitement when you feel borderline invincible. Your body's beginning to heal and you're buoyed up by the support around you – the check-ins from caring friends and family, the praise. You feel like a hero who can take on the world. And it's great. I like

to compare it to getting a positive pregnancy test when you really want a baby. You see the blue line and the world starts to sing. Everything seems brighter, rosier and full of potential. The world is a joyful place and there's no hurdle you can't overcome. Then the baby arrives. It never seems to sleep, and parenthood is not quite the picnic you'd pictured. It's the same with the thrill of sobriety. In the days following your decision, when things are starting to click and you realise you're doing it, actually doing it – you're on a massive high and there's nothing you can't handle. But, gradually, things level out, your adrenaline drops and the inevitable comedown hits. Gone are the constant back-slaps and check ins, and reality resumes. The dreaded "feelings" re-emerge. Because life's challenges, issues and emotions don't just disappear when you're sober. If anything, they become more acute. You can see them more clearly and know they require action. And on top of it, you have to deal with them without your "trusty friend".

It's at this point you might start to stray back towards that old narrative again. In the past you'd have drowned the dreaded feelings with a drink or six, but without that option, it's hard. What do you do with all these feelings? What does "just sit with them" actually mean? It suddenly feels difficult to remember why you gave up drinking in the first place. You dust off those rose-tinted glasses and start thinking "just one can't hurt".

This is where you have to dig deep, give yourself a pep talk and keep yourself going. You could refer back to your list of "whys". Better still, why not write it out and stick it somewhere visible, like the fridge or the bathroom mirror.

Life sober will sometimes feel like you're cycling up a steep hill with no respite. It can feel overwhelming and impossible. Other days you're on a straight, flat path. It can feel a little dull but it's blissfully peaceful. But, more often than not, you get those freewheeling downhill days, where you feel great, and it all seems effortless. Remember to keep pedaling whatever the day. Don't be tempted to chuck your bike in a bush and call an Uber when the hill is steep. You'll only have to go back and retrieve it the following day – hungover, depressed, shame-steeped and livid with yourself. Keep on keeping on, no matter how steep that hill. It's the only way.

Cross-Addiction
This is where you trade one addiction for another. You fill the gap of one drug with a new one. Booze to binge eating, sex to shopping, ganja to gambling. Whatever it is, it's not a good technique and is something to watch out for. In my case, although I stopped drinking, I found myself looking for the next hit because my brain was wired to getting daily doses of external gratification. I started buying trainers. Shitloads of trainers. I felt I could justify it because of the money I was saving on

booze. In fact, I still have a pair in the box unworn and I don't even like them.

I think real self-awareness is key. It's so important to ground yourself when giving up a substance. Avoid things like online gambling adverts for free spins, be mindful of overeating because you "no longer drink" and don't spend money on crap just because you can.

Instead, why not ponder the questions: why do I crave reward? What am I trying to fill? What is it I really need?

Peer Pressure and Sober Socialising
Some friends will be unsettled by your newfound sobriety. Sad but true. They're usually the ones you drank with because it mutually validated your boozy behaviour. "If Dave's having twelve pints, I'm fine on eight". Together you avoided the truth. In the sober light of day, you may find you have nothing in common with these people. You may realise you needed to be pissed with them in order to enjoy the superficial, rowdy banter, and that without alcohol there's not a lot to say.

It can induce feelings of guilt. You feel as though you're abandoning longstanding friendships. But being selfish, in the true sense of the word, is an act of self-love. I felt selfish when I abandoned my persona "Gluggs", but in reality, it was the kindest thing I could do for everyone. Sometimes you owe it to yourself to put yourself first.

If your old crowd are work colleagues who socialise in the pub at lunchtime or after work, make sure you have other plans. Go for a walk or to a bookshop/cafe at lunchtime instead of the pub. Plan other post-work activities, especially at the end of the week, so you're not pressured into the Friday night booze up. There are a million things you can say if you're not ready to declare your intentions – a health kick, weight loss, training for a charity run or perhaps a recent trip to the doctor that indicated high blood pressure. Getting in there first with a solid reason should help curb their alcohol-pushing antics.

You will lose a couple of friends – be prepared for that. But the ones you lose will be gone for a good reason: they're not true friends. You'll get accused of "being boring", but let's be honest, there's nothing more boring than the incoherent, pissed-up pub fly with zero self-awareness who doesn't know when to put a bloody sock in it. And remember that a friend who doesn't have your best interests at heart is not really your friend.

We all have different kinds of friends. The good-time gang, the laugh-a-minute lot, the crisis squad, the party-people, the old timers. Some span one or two of these categories, rare ones span them all. There are the ones who make us laugh but who we'd never call at 3am to "talk". Then there are the ones who are always there for us – no matter what, why or when. It's probably a good idea to identify your core crew –

the reliable, steady ones who genuinely have your best interests at heart. Get them onside early doors with an open and honest conversation about why you're doing what you're doing, and the process will be a lot easier. Then be realistic about which friendships rely solely on drinking. Hard though it may seem, you need to keep your distance from this lot in the early days.

There are some people you can't do this with. Work colleagues or family members perhaps. You need to learn to navigate the inevitable triggers – when they invite you to boozy events or take the piss out of your newfound "boringness". It's about holding the line and restating your boundaries. Just say no to things that no longer serve you. Be polite but firm. Remind people that you're not drinking before an event rather than at it. A simple "I don't drink anymore" or "remember I'm not drinking" usually gets the message over. Don't apologise for it but set your boundaries. Repeating the affirmation "today I will not drink" to yourself is a reminder of your new narrative, your new existence as a non-drinker. If you do encounter any resistance, any tone-deafness or mischief from people who have no idea of the stakes involved or are uncomfortable with their own drinking on some level, then stay calm and restate your boundaries.

One of the best things about going sober is the new friends it brings. You're probably thinking *'But I hate sober people! If someone tells me they're sober at a party, I assume they're either boring or a raving alcoholic and vow to steer clear.'* I know. I thought exactly the same thing. But I promise you, this is just not the case. I've met some of the weirdest, wackiest, brightest, boldest, adventurous, generous and renegade people in the sober community. Don't forget that sober people are sober for a reason. If you look at it another way, they're sober because they are all or nothing people, which means they're exciting and get a kick out of the highs of life. Nothing boring about that.

WHEN THE GOING GETS TOUGH

There will be times when this feels hard. Too hard. But remember that we're humans and humans can do hard things. Here are some thoughts and tips about what to do when the shitteth hitteth the fanneth.

The Power of Human Connection

The shame, stigma and guilt experienced by those in recovery can prevent us reaching out for help. There's often a sense that we've put our loved ones through enough without making more demands on them. But believe me, the people who truly love you are desperate to help – they just need to know how. So don't be afraid to ask.

Asking for what we need is not out of order. Imagine if we could all be open and vulnerable enough to do this on a daily basis. Our needs being discussed and met regularly. We'd all be so much happier! When it comes to recovery, we're already deeply vulnerable as we set about rebuilding our confidence and sense of self, so finding support in whatever capacity is a crucial part of the process. Identify your core team – it may be a family member, close friend or partner. It may be those within an online forum or in-person support group. Whoever you choose, allow yourself to be direct and open with them and you will be rewarded. Human connection is the enemy of addiction, so keep communicating and connecting whatever it takes.

If you have to attend an event but the thought of free-flowing booze makes you feel unsafe, either don't put yourself through it or discuss your feelings with the host. If you're having a down day and need some extra sensitivity from those around you, let them know. It may feel unnatural and uncomfortable, but it's worth it.

Embrace the challenge of your early sobriety journey. It's not a linear path, and your feelings will be up and down like a bride's nightie. Acceptance of that and preparing for the dips, celebrating the highs is all part of your new narrative. Try not to catastrophise if you feel you haven't got a grip on what you're doing from time to time. We tend to make more of the bad days, when nothing seems to go right, and we don't spend enough time feeling pride in our achievements. As if bad stuff counts more than good stuff. The opposite is true. The expression "this too shall pass" is one to live by, and remember, you're learning with every stumble, every climb, you're getting stronger and better equipped.

The Power of Distraction
What the hell are you going to do at 6pm now if you can't have a drink? In the first few weeks of sobriety, you'll battle with your old, ingrained narrative. This is perfectly normal. Human brains are just habit machines, so don't interpret this narrative as doubt. You have made the right decision, and this is the right time to do it! You just need to change things up. You could plan exercise with a mate, go to a class, start or revisit a hobby. It's time to get planning, so grab your journal or a piece of paper and let's get cracking.

Make a list right now of all the things you could do of an evening that don't require alcohol.

Of course, there are whole weekends to navigate now too. So, start thinking about how you want to spend them. What makes you feel good? Going for a run, walk or a game of tennis? A trip to the countryside or the seaside? Watching a movie you love or rereading a favourite book? Hanging out with the kids? Discovering the world of podcasts? There are so many great ones out there, including (*coughs*) *One for the Road*, which will make you feel less alone.

Make a list right now entitled "All the things that make me feel good". Now think about what you have always wanted to do. It could be something major like planning a life-changing trip or running a marathon, or it could be something as simple and rewarding as decluttering the shed or finally painting the spare room. Time for a bucket list.

Warning: May result in feelings of excitement
Revisit these lists whenever you're having a wobble, feeling bored or doubting your decision. The longer and more eclectic the list, the likelier you are to smash through those triggers towards an infinitely happier, healthier you.

Sitting with it
There's no getting away from this phrase, so let's give it some airtime. The truth is, there is incredible power in not distracting yourself. If you find yourself alone and feeling vulnerable, the first thing to do is reach out. Pick up the phone and call or text someone – take yourself out of that fragile interior headspace and feel the strength in sharing how you feel.

The other option is to confront your feelings head on by sitting with them. This is the act of allowing yourself to feel painful emotions rather than pushing them away or smothering them. It is an incredibly empowering thing to do. Why? Because it teaches us that emotions can't actually hurt you. They are just messages. And they are temporary. They surface for a reason, so when they do, notice where they take you. Do you feel childlike? Scared? Anxious? Tell yourself it's okay to feel whatever it is and get curious about how it actually feels. Another great technique is to write the feelings down or record them via voice notes. By acknowledging your emotions, you are listening to yourself, which is not only cathartic, but a big step towards developing the self-compassion you need to succeed.

Go off piste
In the early weeks and months of your sobriety, try and seize all opportunities that will lift you up, motivate you, reinforce your new narrative and boost your self-esteem. This could be a home or garden-based project, voluntary work or planning some sort of adventure/challenge. Or something to get those grey cells going again? An online course in web design or sign language? Something creative, perhaps – cordon bleu cookery class, anyone?!

Pick something you are genuinely interested in or have always wanted to do. Being productive, creative or useful works wonders on your morale, which in turn makes dealing with your emotional landscape easier. One of the best things about sobriety is that it will offer you these opportunities, it opens doors that were closed to you before – doors that you didn't even know existed. Your world gets bigger, brighter and more beautiful every single day.

When I was a few weeks into my own sobriety, I agreed to do something truly terrifying – to give a talk in a pub to loads of drinkers about my experience of alcohol dependence. I remember staring down from the stage at a pint of Peroni, my favourite beer, while I was clutching my lime and soda. I felt so exposed I could have been stark naked, fear churning in my gut at the sight of all those faces. It was a real moment, I was shit-scared and that Peroni looked so good. I was really being tested.

But I did it. I stood there stone-cold sober and talked, and people listened to what I had to say. I saw a few people nod, exchange knowing glances, and I realised that some of them recognised themselves in my story. Afterwards, so many people came up to me and said how inspiring it had been and, honestly, I felt *amazing*. I had seized an opportunity and gone through with it, and it had paid off more than I thought possible. My self-esteem soared that night. Yours can, too.

*'Each body is different
Therefore each rehabilitation must be different.'*

— Joerg Teichmann

RECOVERY: TREATMENT METHODS AND MEDS

When you make the decision to quit drinking for good, you'll need support. There are a variety of options, whether that's a strong community network, therapy, the structured but more spiritual methods offered by Alcoholics Anonymous, or more hardcore and residential private rehabilitation treatment. I have my own views on what methods are the most effective and the cons – even the dangers – of some of them. But each to their own. Only you can ultimately decide what will work best for you, and so being armed with the facts about the treatments on offer should be a priority.

For those with more ingrained and severe AUD, who genuinely want to stop, be aware of how withdrawal and detox will affect you. When your body is used to large amounts of alcohol – more than that, it depends on booze to function – it can go into shock when alcohol is withdrawn and the effect of that can in itself be damaging. It's not a bad idea to get medical advice before you give up. Sometimes, medication is prescribed to combat the effects of withdrawal and help with detoxification, such as the tranquiliser chlordiazepoxide. In more serious cases – for people who drink more than twenty units of alcohol a day – there are specialised clinics that closely monitor and help those suffering physical distress from not drinking. Not everyone needs this help, but some do and for them it can make the difference between relapsing and staying sober in the first days and weeks of recovery.

If you're wondering about what sorts of medication are administered by health professionals (The National Institute for Health and Care Excellence, or NICE for short) to assist alcohol withdrawal, here's a rundown:

Acamprosate (or its brand name, Campral) works to prevent relapse in those who have achieved sobriety by reducing the levels of gamma-amino-butyric acid (GABA) in the brain, since GABA is believed to be influential when it comes to craving alcohol. Acamprosate is generally used in combination with therapy and is administered early on in the withdrawal process and continued for around six months.

Disulfiram (Antabuse) is not dissimilar to Acamprosate in that it prevents relapse, but its process is different and it's more commonly used in those who have already tried and failed to remain sober. What this drug does is act as a deterrent to alcohol use by causing uncomfortable physical responses whenever you drink. Nausea, vomiting, chest pain and dizziness are four unpleasant reactions you might feel if you do succumb to a craving. On this drug it isn't just booze that will trigger a reaction, it is anything that contains alcohol, such as mouthwash, even aftershave, perfume and vinegar. Along with this, it's advisable to avoid substances like paint thinner and other solvents, as these give off alcoholic fumes. But it is effective.

Naltrexone is also used to prevent relapse or to limit the amount you drink. It does this by blocking what are called "opioid receptors" in your body. These receptors enable your response to alcohol, giving you the effects you crave. If they're blocked, then in effect drinking becomes pointless. Naltrexone also blocks the effects of other drugs that contain opioids, including some painkillers.

Another drug, *Nalmefene*, works in a similar way to Naltrexone and is best taken if you don't have any physical withdrawal symptoms and for grey area drinkers who want to cut down on their drinking without necessarily becoming completely abstinent. It is also recommended to be taken in conjunction with therapy.

For everyone else, make yourself aware of how you might react to sudden sobriety and be armed with the information. Disturbed sleep is a common symptom, fluctuating moods, anxiety, fatigue and perhaps generally feeling unwell are others. Withdrawal symptoms will be at their worst during the first forty-eight hours; after that, your body will start to adjust and usually within a month of total abstinence it will have settled down. During the first weeks, make sure you drink plenty of fluids such as water (three litres a day), avoid caffeine and eat a nutritious diet. If you've been given medication to help you, then avoid driving or operating heavy machinery, instead do some gentle exercise, and talk to trusted friends and family. Line up comforting, safe distractions such as TV, books or walks in nature.

Along with help with the physical effects of detoxing and withdrawal, the NHS offers initial therapy or counselling, which is known as "Brief Intervention". This is a short, approximately fifteen-minute counselling session and ideal for grey area drinkers who have become anxious about their use of alcohol and need to talk through the possible reasons behind it, as well as to learn how to wean themselves off their habit. Depending on how much you drink and how much it affects you, you'll also be advised on other longer-term therapy available (some of it may be NHS run and free, though there will be a waiting list). If you're without any other support network or find it difficult to talk to loved ones or friends about how much alcohol affects you, BI is worth considering. It is confidential and trustworthy, though as resources in the NHS are stretched, it may not offer you enough help quickly enough.

If you can afford to pay for private therapy, Cognitive Behavioural Therapy (CBT) is the most common type offered to addicts. First designed to clinically manage mood disorders, CBT has been adapted over time to treat addiction in general. CBT operates on the theory that certain negative thought patterns are strong contributors to maladaptive behaviour such as prolonged substance abuse. A CBT practitioner will help you identify the thoughts and emotions that compel you to drink as they come up and understand their origins. The more you understand what motivates these thoughts, the better equipped you are to change their pattern, and replace anxiety-fuelled cravings with healthier and more positive thoughts and behaviour. CBT is considered by many to be a broadly effective therapy because it sets you up for managing your mental health long-term and its benefits remain long after you've achieved sobriety. Because it is helping you navigate and manage your emotions, it improves self-esteem, productivity and relationships. Options for CBT practice include individual as well as group therapy, and work you can do at home using the techniques you've learned.

Another type of therapy is Dialectical Behavioural Therapy (DBT), which was developed for practice in the States but has fairly recently been implemented in Europe. Dominantly used for treating more specific (and often more severe) mental health disorders such as borderline personality disorder, DBT is a more hardcore version of CBT, and has a more rigorous, structured treatment schedule, focusing on the root of debilitating mental health and addressing grave impulses, such as suicidal thoughts and more immediately dangerous self-harming behaviour. It's only in its infancy this side of the pond and unlikely to be offered on the NHS, but if your addiction and its root is of the more tenacious and crippling variety and you can afford it, it is worth investigating as a treatment method.

Alcoholics Anonymous, which uses the 12-Step method as a belief system to support anyone in recovery from alcohol abuse, is probably the most well-known of the treatment methods. AA encourages abstinence through a structure of regular meetings where members meet and participate in sharing experiences and feelings around their drinking. The 12-Step method runs on a three-part mantra:

- Acceptance – accept that you are powerless over alcohol, that it has made your life unmanageable and that your willpower alone is not enough to overcome your addiction. Instead, you draw on a "higher power" to help you maintain sobriety.
- Surrender – members must surrender to this higher power to combat what is seen as "the disease" of addiction.
- Abstinence – unsurprisingly, you are held accountable for your sobriety. If you fall off the

wagon, you publicly declare it to the group and to the higher power.

12-step facilitation therapy is recommended for those who don't feel comfortable sharing their feelings and experiences in a group setting. Instead, you work through the stages of sobriety on a one-to-one basis with a trained counsellor.

Millions around the world draw comfort and motivation from their AA attendance, and the meeting forum itself, where experiences are shared and camaraderie gives people a valuable sense of belonging, and crucially within that framework diminishes stigma and shame around their drinking. There is a lot about what AA offers that is positive and nurturing. The fact that there is a meeting on any day of the week in towns and cities all over the world means you are never far away from your sobriety community, and the rules and structure around the 12-Step method offers many people much-needed stability. What's more, meetings are populated by folk of all ages and from all different walks of life. From royalty to refuse collectors, inside the sanctity of the meeting, you are all equal. You are also allotted a sponsor – a kind of mentor who has been sober for a sufficient number of years, who is there as a kind of buddy-coach hybrid, someone to turn to when you're feeling shaky and in need of a pep talk. Again, many find it comforting to have a guardian of this kind. Belonging to this broad and inclusive network really does provide the belonging that so many people need to motivate them day in and day out.

My own feelings around AA and its methodology have been conflicted. Very early on in my own recovery, I was really interested in this programme, which has undeniably supported so many through sobriety and effectively helped them maintain it. I went along to my first meetings and was overwhelmed by the warmth, offers of sponsorship and welcoming attitude. I was presented with the "big book" on the twelve steps that all members are given, and my impression was of a church-like experience, a cocoon of love and acceptance. I was love-bombed by potential sponsors who wanted to mentor me through my first steps as a non-drinker, and ended up giving my number out to several of them – each of them wasting no time in offering me one-to-one support. One guy was on the phone to me for an hour, and by the end of the call I felt quite drained by the intensity of it all. I'd gone from being a secretive, often introverted hardened boozer whose emotions rarely touched the sides, to someone who was expected to share the depths of his soul to a virtual – albeit very kind and well-meaning – stranger.

I quickly felt stressed by what was expected of me. AA has its rules, as mentioned earlier, quite rightly there to create boundaries and stability for those in recovery, with consequences for not toeing the line. I remember casually mentioning that I was going camping and taking a couple of non-alcoholic beers with me and was met with extreme disapproval. My hackles went up at the inflexibility of this "church" I had wandered into, and the more childish part of me didn't want to be told what to do. I think in a way I was panicking. Not only was I trying to stay off the booze, but I also had to stay within guidelines I didn't quite understand; I had to be "good". The sheer amount of "listening" to others' stories was draining; I had so much crashing around in my own head that I didn't feel I had room for anyone else's experience. In the meetings I went to, often the same people spoke each time, and told the same old stories over and over again. One had been clean and going to meetings for thirty years. In resistance mode, I couldn't understand what good it was doing to stay stuck in the same place, with the same story.

The pressure made me a bit petulant and resentful, and I was convinced I could do better on my own. It was arrogant of me, a sobriety novice, to dismiss the benefits of this confessional support-forum for millions in recovery. I couldn't buy into the spiritual element, but it works incredibly well for those who need faith in something beyond themselves to feel hope, and to prevent relapsing. And for so many people, being seen and listened to is a lifeline. Since then, I have found a method of sobriety that works for me, and throwing myself into my coaching and mentoring work really helps me keep in touch with the highs and lows, the daily affirmations, and the conversations that keep me from being complacent. Who knows, without the vocation I have as Soberdave, I might well return to the 12-Step AA method. I certainly feel more humbled by the incredible service it provides.

SMART Recovery. An acronym for self-management and recovery training, SMART recovery's approach to alcohol rehabilitation is that by channelling self-empowerment, addiction can be overcome, along with destructive behavioural patterns. It differs from the 12-Step programme (with its spiritual foundations) by implementing more practical cognitive behavioural therapy and motivational techniques.

SMART's ethos is that addiction is a choice and *not* a disease, and centres its techniques around solid scientific knowledge, regularly adapting to the evolution of that science. In other words, it very much puts the power in the hands of the recovering addict to be taught how to overcome their addiction without a higher power being instrumental to that process. It educates people on how to develop self-reliance, backed up by a four-point programme, which works by treating participants as individuals with specific needs around their behaviour, so a tailored approach rather than the more one-size-fits-all of the 12-Step.

How does the four-point programme work?

- Building and maintaining motivation by asking its members to list their priorities and the pros and cons of sobriety versus continued addictive behaviour.

- It educates on how to cope with and suppress cravings and behavioural urges by going into the science behind them, such as what stimulates them, and by teaching the power of distraction techniques.
- Members learn how to manage their thoughts, feelings and behaviours by self-exploration and self-acceptance. Understanding what motivates and fulfills needs and removing self-judgement, improving self-esteem.
- SMART training promotes healthy maintenance of sobriety by teaching how to set realistic goals in recovery and planning for a future without alcohol.

REHAB

Now we come to what is often known as "rehab". A pretty casual label for an AUD treatment option that caters to the rich and often famous and is often eye-wateringly expensive. The luxury spa-type branding of these places invites vulnerable people with lots of money to either a residential hotel experience, a luxury spa with meds and therapy, or private outpatient clinics with all the anonymity that provides.

You could argue that when someone chooses private alcohol rehab over less costly treatment that they are giving themselves premium care and an experience that is more like a vacation than rehabilitation with the kind of bespoke treatment plan they deserve, promising:

- Individual care with attentive focus to a client's needs, personalised treatment plans and targeted therapy.
- Tailored treatment and therapy programmes in individual or small group settings. Many private rehab centres have a limited intake of clients to promote exclusivity and more intimate, personalised care and connection between clients and staff.
- A variety of programme options for all kinds of ages, sexualities and needs, from teenagers to same-sex facilities, all with the aim of making each client feel seen and special.

WHAT ARE THE TWO PRIVATE ALCOHOL REHAB VARIETIES?

Although no two private rehab centres are the same, there are essentially two different kinds:

- Inpatient rehab is a residential programme where clients can have a private room, eat gourmet meals, and receive all bespoke treatments and therapies while staying there. Private inpatient services promise the seclusion and support a person needs to focus completely on rehabilitation from their addiction to alcohol. One benefit of this is that the patient is entirely removed from their usual environment and negative drinking patterns are easier to break.

- Outpatient alcohol rehab is designed for those who have commitments (children, or a job they need to be visible in) but need consistent support and the confidentiality that comes with that. This is a good choice for those who want to juggle everyday life with sobriety support and retain anonymity. You can literally pay for your own private rehab schedule, but you do have to contend with the temptation to drink that staying in your familiar environment may trigger. Outpatient rehab is better for grey area drinkers, or those whose addiction is less severe.

Other than the luxury surroundings and the more soft-focus approach, private rehab will provide exactly the same methods as NHS treatment – detox and withdrawal support, the use of medication to assist the recovery process and therapy. But here there is no waiting list, and there is the illusion of glamour, with meditation and yoga, swimming pools, tennis, holistic centres, massage, acupuncture and aromatherapy on tap to help with the healing process.

To me, there are issues with many of the often well-known rehab centres that make me doubtful of a genuine ambition to really help their patients achieve lasting sobriety. Is it in their interests that people fully recover, after all? The cynic in me thinks they get richer on the failure of the vulnerable people who come to them for a set period and are then turfed out to fend for themselves. Private rehab centres don't provide proper aftercare, which is essential in my mind. Patients might connect with a counsellor or therapist during their rehab, but have that abruptly cut short when they leave; left to adjust to everyday life and all its triggers with little armoury. Maybe I'm too much of a cynic, but with the recent controversy surrounding some of these high-profile rehab centres, it is absolutely vital if you do want to go down this route that you rigorously do your research. Search for positive testimonials, sure, but also for any less than glowing reviews.

PRIVATE ONE-TO-ONE COACHING AND MENTORING

This is allied with "outpatient rehab" in as much as it's private and there are fees to pay, but it is designed to fit around everyday life, and the choice is yours as to how regularly you attend sessions and for how long. It is beneficial for those who need to "check in" with themselves and any negative behaviour patterns they have adopted with alcohol, but do not have a habit that is as yet affecting their ability to function at work or in relationships – grey area drinkers, for example. Like a check-up to help reset and motivate those who feel they're straying into excess. That's not to say that the more hardcore drinkers won't achieve results from this type of work, but since there are fees attached, they'll have to have deep pockets. As an accredited coach myself, helping all kinds of people from all walks of life, I recommend this to strengthen and support your core psyche, much as hiring a personal trainer would benefit your core muscle strength, but checking out qualifications is vital. Read up on feedback and results when looking for the right coach for you and don't just pick the first service that pops up in a Google search. Compare prices, too. Make sure you can afford it, and that it's worth the money.

'Whenever there is a challenge, there is also an opportunity to face it, to demonstrate and develop our will and determination.'

— the Dalai Lama

HITTING WALLS

Hitting walls – confronting life challenges that affect your drinking or your sobriety – are a fact of life. In conquering addictive behaviour, these challenges are all part of the rediscovery process. As I touched on in the Choosing Sobriety chapter, accommodating this fact as part of your preparation to go sober is vital. Hitting a sobriety wall and managing to get over, under or round it, brings growth, learning and strength, though it's important to remember that failure to do this also brings wisdom, if you can be kind enough to yourself to let it. Failure is an important part of anyone's journey through life, whether they're an addict or not. In fact, failing can be one of the most significant parts of success. With every decision you make, good or bad, there is an opportunity to learn something. Using failure as a reason to sink back into self-loathing, to give up or give in, is the killer. As hard it might seem, picking yourself up without judgement and moving forward is an act of bravery.

One important thing we need to know in recovery is that factoring in challenging times and situations and preparing your armoury in the face of them is a key part of your emotional toolbox. Like an insurance policy you pay into, it limits the damage when destabilising events come round the corner. Preparation means you are not complacent, you have contingency plans.

When you're in recovery, maybe still high on the pink cloud not long after you've made the big decision to quit drinking, and when the spotlight is on you, your resolve is iron-fast. Your determination to escape that abusive relationship you've been in is strong. You might feel a kind of invincibility. Sobriety feels fresh and new, the people around you are lifting you up with support. All good, except that when you're standing on that safe plateau, feeling the waves of encouragement all around you, the sharp edges of your addiction can begin to soften the safer you feel. You are, in a sense, lulled into a false sense of security.

Stopping drinking is like ending a toxic relationship with an abusive partner, there is a euphoria in having made the break, in finally escaping, and comfort comes from people who care about you cheering on your decision. You are carried along by the approval you're getting, and you start to feel more capable and strong. You might even feel you're home and dry, you've ripped off the addiction plaster, and now everything will be all right.

But nothing worth doing is that easy. It's a tough one, and though it's true to say that some will find sobriety easier to maintain than others, no one gets away without hitting walls. Life will present you with challenges because that's what life does, and some of those challenges will really test you. Taken in isolation, some of these challenges are benign: holidays, Christmas, a lads' or girls' weekend away to a festival, a stag or a hen night, a birthday do… Traditionally, for many, these are "celebrations", times to kick back and let your hair down, over-indulge for a while. And for them, no harm is done and afterwards normal life resumes.

Not so for those in any stage of sobriety. These events threaten you, they throw you off your recovery game. There is dread: how am I going to get through this without a drink? Whether it's a major trauma or an upcoming challenging event, the prospect of having to decline alcohol and spend hours watching everyone around you get pissed can be too much to bear. Or the prospect of talking to people sober is too intimidating. Beware the tricks your brain can play on you when these walls appear in front of you. If you have drifted back into a mindset where you view the past through rose-tinted glasses, giving into your addiction may be dangerously tempting. Like the abusive ex who could be sweet and loving sometimes, alcohol can seduce you back. What would be the harm in seeing them one more time? This delusional thinking is a form of running away from reality.

For those who are not yet on the sobriety path, some of the above applies, but the difference is that while you're still drinking you don't even question whether you're going to use alcohol to get through that wedding, or funeral, or stag weekend, it's a given. It's so much easier to be a drunk than a sober alcoholic. If you remove the bigger picture, the future where you've lost everything, you look like shit and your liver's packed up, then it's a no-brainer to carry on boozing.

f   My difficult relationship with alcohol really started when my husband Greg was diagnosed with terminal bowel cancer in 2016. I was living at the hospital, and our two small children were living at my parents ... I was so petrified, so wired, so living in another world. I would take two sleeping pills with a glass of wine when I got home ... I was desperately trying to knock myself out from a very, very nightmarish situation, and I think that's when it started to become a little bit of a crutch for me. I had post-natal depression, and I felt like our lives were falling apart. I definitely fell into that whole "wine o'clock" thing.

It was at the beginning of lockdown that there was 360 turn on my drinking. Greg was three years into his diagnosis, and had been about to start chemo on the 23rd of March, but his treatment was then cancelled indefinitely. As a family, we just shut up shop, having to rely on other people to bring us food ... and when they brought us food, they also brought us alcohol. The drink of choice was Prosecco. I was at home with bottles and bottles of alcohol. We did nothing but sit around, and I was sitting around drinking Prosecco. It was blocking out the harsh reality of what was going on, the madness of being home with small children. I also used alcohol to pretend I was somewhere else, that this was something other than a global pandemic with my terminally ill husband and my two small children. I became really aware of how much I was drinking, but I didn't vocalise it to Greg because I didn't want him to try to stop it,

if I'm honest. I really did enter my own little bubble …
hiding bottles that came into the house, then hiding the
empty bottles, then the glasses I was drinking out of. It
became acceptable to have Prosecco at 10am … and
I had absolutely no interest in doing anything about it.

)

Stacey Heale

Earlier this year, in 2022, I came up against a wall – a pretty big one – one that I'm still facing. Sadness, conflict, turmoil are all major players, and I am dealing with both my own pain and the pain of someone I care for deeply. It's the kind of situation that a few years ago I would have avoided confronting by making sure I was drunk enough not to properly acknowledge my feelings, or theirs. The halcyon days of self-medication!

That's not to say I am out of the woods. When you're in recovery, being aware of your vulnerability is key, and it's a mistake to take your sobriety for granted, something that became clear to me three months into my sobriety back in 2019. I was walking on Wandsworth Common with my dog Lola and I looked over to the pub I used to frequent back in my drinking days; the pub I would fill my boots in until closing time, then leave and pick up more bottles of booze from the shop, usually opening one while I was walking home and drinking it before I got there. It's a version of myself I've long said goodbye to, but back then, in the early months of sobriety, before Soberdave had been conceived, I was just at the point where I was coming down off the pink cloud I'd been floating on, and enjoying all the attention and the encouragement I'd received when I announced I was quitting alcohol. Gradually, people had stopped regularly giving me the thumbs up, patting me on the back for making such a "brave" decision; they had gone back to getting on with their lives, leaving me to it. Though I was trying to build a community of people in recovery, like me, it was early doors, and I was yet to find my real place amongst these beautiful people that I have now. I felt on my own and I had to fend for myself.

Maybe, on some level, coming off the pink cloud gave me a sense of being abandoned all over again. After all, a newly sober person is not dissimilar to a child – a kind of innocence is reborn, along with sensitivity, and it's as though every emotion is brand new – like you're experiencing them all for the first time. When you've spent decades not *feeling* your feelings properly, it makes total sense that you'll feel exposed and fragile when you start to. But I had made a vow to myself that I would never drink again, and I intended to stick with it. That didn't mean that a part of me wasn't grieving a little. I'll bring up my analogy of the abusive ex that you finally find the courage to leave, but still have an occasional unhealthy, lingering affection for, even though you know you'll never go back to them.

It was the first wall I'd encountered, the first time I felt the reality of quitting the booze. It was weird and scary, but that day on the common, looking at my old boozer with its lovely beer garden, I had a moment of saying goodbye to Gluggs and then turning away from him.

I managed to escape colliding with any major walls for nearly a year after that, until March 2020, when the COVID pandemic arrived and the government started talking about lockdown, which became a bitter-sweet experience for me.

To be fair, a large percentage of the country hit a wall around March 2020. The prospect of severely restricted freedom, where everything shut down, and we were shut inside, allowed out twice a day to the shops and for exercise, working from home, or not being able to work, spending all day every day with your partner and kids, or spending all day alone with just yourself for company – it was a lot to get your head around, even if you had no addictions. For those attempting sobriety or in recovery from any addiction, it was massively triggering… a real danger zone. A few thoughts went through my head back then, when supermarket queues and panic-buying bog roll were rife. First: 'Thank God I don't drink anymore, how the hell would I have managed to get my booze supplies in secret?' Then, when lockdown moved from hypothetical to a reality: 'Oh, God, I don't drink anymore, how am I going to cope without all the distractions I need?' Added to that were worries about my livelihood (my carpet-fitting business) and money, or the lack of it. And finally, home-schooling. Not being a natural academic myself, trying to help three kids with their schoolwork was a prolonged exercise in humiliation for me! The whole thing amounted to a recipe for relapse, a really challenging time for everyone who'd relied on a certain set of circumstances to keep their heads above water.

Fortunately, my resourcefulness kicked in, because

2020 was the year I took the first proper steps to building my coaching up. My Instagram account was well established and, by posting and sharing my journey, it began to draw people going through recovery themselves to a safe, inclusive place where support and motivation to keep going was on offer. I started to gain a following, a refuge for many in the midst of an isolated existence and an uncertain future. I channelled the challenge, I broke through the wall by turning my predicament and my sobriety into a tool for others, to try and help them stay afloat. When the podcast was born in early 2021, I realised how lucky I was to have paddled my way through tough waters. I say "lucky" because not everyone is able to tap into creativity as a way of coping with challenge.

Since Soberdave took off, I've come up against more walls, more periods of intense discomfort and relationship struggles, and some situations have not eased. But one of the good things about experience and getting older is that you know feelings come and go, that just adopting one or two techniques that work for you can change the way you feel enough for you to keep going and not crave your old crutches.

COPING WITH MAJOR LIFE EVENTS WITHOUT BOOZE

When we experience major life events or shocks, we often initially cope by dealing with the practical issues around them and by talking to friends and relatives, which provide distraction from the high drama that comes with a profoundly traumatic experience. The fact is that the pain is still there, waiting to come out, but for now, you are cushioned by the love and attention you're getting. Whether you are in recovery or still drinking, you are vulnerable.

The big life events: divorce, bereavement, redundancy, bankruptcy, serious illness (yours or someone else's), these traumas are a whole different level – not one-offs, not celebrations, often lengthy. Coming up against any of these, whether you are in sobriety or not, may very reasonably make you want to reach for your trusty anaesthetic after a while. It's so easy to let these challenges feed into your negative narrative about yourself and your life. That good things just aren't meant for you, maybe even that you deserve what's happening to you, and that trying to change anything is pointless. Life is unfair, we know this, but it hasn't singled you out, it isn't personal, but how you manage your life and what it throws up is personal. You are the only one who can navigate your way through these difficult times, but to do this you will need help. Whether that is counselling or therapy, AA meetings, good friends, or meditation, your job is to recognise that you need help and to ask for it. This means making yourself vulnerable, which if you've spent a lifetime avoiding it, is hard.

Through my work as a recovery coach, and

simply by talking to people who are in sobriety, or have been, there is a pattern when it comes to certain triggering events. There is dread, maybe even panic and then there is confidence. These can dangerously combine. You're unable to face the situation and all the awkwardness, pain and difficulty that comes with it. Besides, you've been really good… you haven't had a drink for a month. You can do it! What harm will one drink do, just to take the edge off? In fact, don't you deserve it? Like the diet where you lose half a stone, then reward yourself with a massive burger and fries and some sticky toffee pudding. It's an irrational mindset, triggered by a bizarre kind of high. The high you get when you've made the decision to have a drink (or eat the massive burger), but you haven't done it yet. You exist for a while in a dopamine bubble, looking forward to that drink, maybe even telling yourself that you can back out if you want to. Telling yourself you are in control.

It's important to recognise also that, for the same reason you stay in an abusive relationship, comfort and familiarity plays a big part in retreating to that version of yourself, the helpless addict, when it feels like too much is required of you. You might feel angry: "why should I have to do this?" Or just simply: "I don't like change". It's hard to change, it's hard to be without your crutch. It's lonely sometimes. And there are many times you might feel "what's the point? I'm miserable anyway. At least alcohol took the edge off that".

Wanting to reach for a drink is essentially you running away from your feelings. Until you can learn to sit with those feelings, experience them with clarity and, yes, pain, and come out the other side, you are always going to be in a high-risk zone whenever situations threaten to bring them up.

Again, keeping a note of how you feel, day to day if possible, through journalling is a good way of expressing your feelings. A good therapist can also be invaluable, but if you can't afford one, or are stuck on a waiting list for one through the NHS, you'll need to be your own therapist. Besides, getting into the daily habit of being present with your emotions is you keeping a check on yourself; like a regular *Columbo*, develop your detective skills around your behaviour. Get to know yourself.

Visualisation helps. I think of the traffic lights model when encountering a "wall". Green, amber and red. Green is when there is equilibrium, you aren't facing a triggering situation, you feel stable, and sobriety is doable. Amber is when that challenge looms, and so does anxiety; this is when you're likely to start thinking of ways to avoid this challenge, bypass it. Red is when you're teetering on the cliff edge, maybe you've gone out and bought yourself a bottle of your booze of choice, you're in the real danger zone. Thinking of this traffic lights model, again in your journal, note down what is coming up for you as you feel it. If you're experiencing discomfort or panic (amber) then expressing it will lift some of it away. If you get into the habit of noting these things down, you are less likely to reach red. It's amazing how self-awareness can work as a pre-emptive strike.

I can't stress enough how valuable your emotional toolbox is, and how you should carry it with you wherever you go. Sobriety is a one-day-at-a-time process, every day is different, and there are some tools you'll need to pull out regularly. As I touched on right at the beginning of this chapter, knowing and stating your boundaries is vital, a sign of self-respect and good mental health. But, in order to know what your boundaries are, you need to know who *you* are. What values you hold, what inspires and makes you happy and what doesn't serve you.

When it was put to me during therapy that I was unsure of my identity, my instant reaction was indignation, anger. But I let myself process this suggestion and realised there was truth in it. When I was drinking, I spent decades shapeshifting, being a slightly different version of myself depending on who I was with or where. In the pub with my fellow drinkers, I was Gluggs – lairy and jovial. At work, I was "Dave the Carpet" – hardworking, professional. If I was in the company of a doctor or a lawyer, I'd summon a more serious, thoughtful side. They were all acts in one way or another. I took on the mantle of whoever I was with. I was so used to acting that my true identity – quiet, sensitive, lost, wanting love and security – was buried. The truth is, getting to know myself is something I am still working on. An ongoing process that I owe myself that I could never have done while I was in the grip of addiction. Back when I was drinking, I was running as far away from myself as I could. I couldn't have told you what made me happy or unhappy, what I wanted, what future I dreamed of, I just lurched from one day to the next, with my constant supply of booze. It has only been in sobriety that I can see my identity with more clarity, and now I'm like a fifty-something crossed with a newborn baby, blinking and full of wonder at the world around me.

Don't be afraid to be vulnerable and to learn. Don't be afraid to fail – failure is there to show you something useful. Don't use difficulty and discomfort with what you're facing as an excuse not to try.

The amazing thing is that whatever you are facing, there is always a support group or forum to join and share your experience. Keep your toolbox close, keep writing in your journal, and turn to your recovery family.

*'Some of us think holding on makes us strong,
but sometimes it is letting go.'*

— Herman Hesse

ADDICTION, RECOVERY AND RELATIONSHIPS

It doesn't take a genius to work out that maintaining relationships while you're in the grip of addiction is difficult. The effects of your drinking – like throwing a pebble in still waters, and watching the ripples it creates – are not confined to you. For anyone who loves or cares for you, it's a painful thing to observe, and it stretches the limits of love to the furthest point. They go through it with you. Hypervigilance, anxiety and dread are part of their lives, along with anger and resentment. The chapter on Children of Alcoholics focuses on a particular relationship – parent and child – and is an area that cannot be talked about enough for the lifetime struggle that COAs experience. But what about those other significant bonds we have? Partners, husbands and wives, siblings and cousins, our own parents, our friends. How do those relationships survive the roller-coaster ride of your addiction? And just as importantly, how can we navigate these same relationships in sobriety?

To try and understand this, we need to go back to how an addiction or dependency on any substance has an impact on our emotional brain. In my case, it numbed me to feelings I didn't want to experience as well as depriving me of the joy of real intimacy. It was a price I was clearly willing to pay for too long. The love of my life was in fact contained in a bottle, and it came first. Sure, as I have recounted, there were periods of "relative" sobriety… in that I might curb my drinking for a few weeks or months, sometimes years, and in those times I would function enough in a relationship to keep it going. I did not, however, ever address the origins of my addiction… what made me want to drown my sorrows. So, I had no contingency plan, no toolkit to really find my way out of that dark tunnel I was in. Maybe I'd see the light at the end of it, but I'd never quite make it as far as the way out. Often, at the first sign of difficulty or conflict, I would turn to my old friend alcohol to make it all go away. A circle of self-destruction that left a trail of failed romances and marriages.

It doesn't take a rocket scientist to work out that events and my experiences of relationships in my childhood and adolescence influenced my own behaviour in relationships. My childhood sweetheart Michelle symbolised safety and became the centre of my world, with her close, lively family and her own maternal warmth, she gave me what I had never really experienced from my mum – affection and devotion –

and I was more than happy to reciprocate, oblivious to the codependency developing between us, and basking in belonging. That need to belong was an addiction in itself, a forerunner to the other, darker and more destructive addiction I was to develop. Understandable that at that age I desperately wanted the pain to go away. The pain of Mum leaving, the pain of Mum never having really been there… at least not in the way I craved. I was still basically a kid with some growing up to do, and I enjoyed the cocoon of that first love with Michelle, though in times to come I developed the beginnings of what was to be a pattern.

See, as much as I craved love, the part of me that was conditioned to believe that, deep down, I was not lovable would ultimately reject anyone who seemed to offer love, who accepted and valued me. As I grew into my later teens, and my more rebellious streak kicked in, I left Michelle behind and courted a more hedonistic single life. I spent a couple of decades ping-ponging between wanting stability and mistrusting it (or sabotaging it). All the while, I stoppered the loneliness and feelings of being lost with intermittent hard drinking, usually calming down when a new woman came on the scene. What I never did was try life without a crutch. Alcohol gave me the confidence to feel attractive and a little bit invincible maybe. It smoothed out the jagged edges of my feelings, but they were always still there, up in that metaphorical suitcase in the loft, yet to be unpacked and looked at.

After a period of my twenties when I'd been larging it, hanging out with my more boisterous friends, partying, when I was young, fit and good-looking, I met Joanna. I was on a lads-only holiday in Greece, and Joanna was one of the holiday reps. She was a bit older, glamorous and a laugh, and we enjoyed a blissful holiday romance, in between my hanging out with my friends. Having had a succession of casual flings with other women and now in a period of moderate boozing, I felt I was ready for something more substantial, and Joanna felt like the one. Missing her friends and family back home, Joanna had made the decision to pack in her job and return to England before my holiday was over, and being young and immature, I almost put the kibosh on any future for us when I failed to turn up on her last day to say goodbye. True, we'd arranged to meet at six in the morning, which was ambitious given I'd probably not got to bed before five, and Joanna did forgive me. In fact, we kept in touch, and as soon I got back from Greece, we started a relationship. It was impulsive on my part – one of many irrational decisions I made without thinking about it – and Joanna moved in with me quickly. She was tee-total and because at that time I wasn't drinking a lot – a new relationship seemed to have staved off the habit – I did what any codependent with self-esteem issues who is keen not to face up to reality does, I launched myself into the intensity of the situation and got pulled along by that. I really liked Joanna, that was real, but it moved too quickly, and then she got pregnant. Our son was born when I was thirty. I was suddenly hit by the responsibility of having a child. Don't get me wrong, there's no way I regret becoming a father to my son, and can't imagine my life without him in it, but I had landed on a major life milestone without, not to put too fine a point on it, sorting my shit out. Joanna was and is an amazing mum, a natural. She was stable and mature and almost completely responsible for how my son has grown up to be an awesome human being. And though I felt a bit in over my head, I also felt a kind of safety in my relationship, safe enough to start drinking again, which doubled up as a handy release from the pressure of being a good-enough dad, I suppose. Since she didn't drink, Joanna didn't take well to my newly resurrected habit, even pouring booze down the drain.

Work was going well for me, however, and we moved to a bigger place, a rented house in Carshalton, where I upped my daily intake of alcohol, getting regularly pissed inside, but hiding the evidence by throwing the empties into the convenient coal bunker in the back garden. I was in trouble but didn't want to face it. One of the tipping points came when, home alone with the baby while Joanna was out, I got so drunk I didn't hear him crying upstairs, and she arrived back to find the poor baby in distress. I still can't think about that without feeling shame.

Inevitably, it signalled the end of my relationship with Joanna, who hadn't signed up for life with an immature alcoholic. I was thirty-two and living a double life – on one side was a partner and father, on the other was Gluggs from the pub. Gluggs won. And Gluggs carried on winning for a while. Like the mistress in a marriage, the forbidden love that lured me out of what could have been a healthy, functioning relationship and into a familiar place, where I wasn't asked to step up, or be accountable, I didn't have to risk being hurt.

The pattern was always the same. I'd vow never to see the mistress again, full of self-loathing and despair, but she – *alcohol* – always had the power to pull me back to her. Like getting a flirtatious text, I couldn't resist.

After Joanna and I split up, I moved out so that she and our son could stay in the flat, and pretty much lived out of my van, drinking solidly and sleeping on a mate's sofa if I could find one available. At some point, I started a relationship with Jessica who worked down the local pub, flatteringly twelve years younger than me, and up for fun. I was besotted with her, and I was free from the full-time restraints of family life and responsibility. It was also pushing me further away from the truth and any self-exploration. As long as I could surround myself with people who demanded nothing but my booze-fuelled company, I was fine. And my drinking was worse than ever. I'd get up early but start drinking at midday until Jessica got back from her shift at the pub in the evenings. We'd then go out clubbing, by which time I was already well pissed.

Not surprisingly, my appeal started to wear off for

Jessica when she realised I was actually permanently drunk, and she moved on.

So, for sure, alcohol has ruined some of my relationships. It wasn't until I started a new relationship that I got properly scared about what I had to lose. I was still drinking then, as I've talked about before, and she went into the relationship not fully aware of my problem, until we moved in together, when it became trickier to conceal. But because I wasn't honest with her about the extent of my drinking, she unwittingly colluded with me. We'd go for weekends away, where a look round the shops was followed by a long lunch – me on the beer, her on the wine. And quite often the rest of the day became a blur as she subconsciously attempted to catch up with me. For every glass of wine she drank, I drank at least a pint. By the time she was on her second glass, I was four or five pints down. We'd return from our weekends hungover, all driven by me. If she was drinking, she didn't notice my excess as much.

Learning how not to drink with a partner who still drinks is tough, and vice versa. If you're the sober one, it's hard to be around alcohol, and if you're the other half then there is a discomfort or guilt at openly drinking when your partner isn't, not to mention that you're getting to know a new person. It wasn't easy, and her love and patience I will be forever grateful for, but I had, and still have, a way to go in my recovery before I can say I am successful in relationships.

It's a big ask of anyone to stay stable and loving when their significant other is closed off to them. Either morose and uncommunicative, or aggressive and unreliable, secretive, emotionally avoidant, in pain. And, honestly, for many who find themselves shacked up with an addict, the advice might be to run. Partners need to take care of their own emotional needs and are responsible for their own happiness. Living with an alcoholic is like bashing your head against a wall again and again. It just keeps on hurting. And if you add kids into the mix, the imperative to provide security for them should come first.

One looming aspect of addiction is that when we are trapped in it, our real sense of self, our identity is either diminished or non-existent. Our emotional brain shrinks to contend with one priority: our next fix. Everything else is blurred, including our hopes and dreams, our capacity for love and for true intimacy. In fact, the idea of intimacy can be terrifying. If we are really known and understood, then we will be rejected, won't we? Who will love us when we don't love ourselves? Well, good point. It would take a psychic saint to see the value in us when we don't. This often dire lack of self-esteem also means we might gravitate towards partners who struggle with their own sense of worth. Maybe we feel we can get away with more. Maybe we feel that they are what we deserve. Damage attracts damage. Nobody who properly values themselves would want us, after all.

The hard truth is that there is a lot of truth in that when it comes to a central, sexual or romantic relationship. Whereas other kinds of relationships, those with our children, brothers or sisters, parents, even close friends, operate on different motivational markers. They are bound with us by flesh and blood, or an innate sense of responsibility. Childhood friends may feel a bond that transcends our behaviour, they may stick around longer, there for the bad times, along with the good. But every single relationship we have while we are in addiction will be tested, and many do not survive the test.

So, the landscape of a functioning relationship for an alcoholic is strewn with difficulty. It is often a shadow of a real relationship, in which both parties collude with each other to avoid the truth. The non-addict may turn away from what they don't want to see. They may cling on to the better times and convince themselves that the bad times are bearable. They may make constant excuses for their other half, even to their children. They will put up with emotional or physical abuse, and like a punchball, they bounce back each time, but each time they are diminished. Eventually, they may be so worn down that they wouldn't have the strength to leave, even if they wanted to. It's almost as if they are as addicted as their partner, if not to alcohol, then to pain. In the chapter Children of Alcoholics, I talk about how kids who've grown up with an alcoholic parent often subconsciously choose an alcoholic partner in adult life. It's a familiar dynamic for them. In a perverse way, it is comforting, even if it is a trap.

Grim, yeah? But what about sobriety in relationships? What about kicking your addiction in an ongoing relationship? Or entering a new relationship in recovery? Seems like this wouldn't be an issue, maybe. But thinking that success is guaranteed simply because you don't drink anymore is a mistake made by many people.

In sobriety, in many ways you experience a rebirth. Sounds a bit woo-woo, but you are undoing often decades of conditioning that is ingrained. Not only in terms of the need to drink, but also the way you see yourself and your place in the world. Your value. Your lovability. Your dreams and ambitions, and what truly makes you happy. It is not uncommon for a radical change of lifestyle to cause discontent in an existing relationship. You are not the same person, after all. You are the butterfly that has emerged from the caterpillar's cocoon, colours shining, and that can be hard on a partner who, as much as they wished you'd give up, is at best startled, at worst made uncomfortable by this stranger they see before them. Weirdly, a new resentment might kick in. Earlier, I talked about how addicts often find themselves involved with partners who lack self-esteem, and for whom your dirty little habit somehow matches their own sense of worthlessness. Well, when their partner gets sober, where does that leave them? It may be that with the "obstacle" of your addiction removed, they feel exposed and vulnerable, ill-equipped to deal with this "better" version of you. And you, newborn into sobriety, may look at them differently. Perhaps the only thing that kept you together was codependency. You needed them, and they needed to be needed. We constantly make decisions in life based on our needs. When our needs change, then new decisions are made, including about who we want in our lives.

The same goes, to an extent, with platonic relationships, which I talk about in the Choosing Sobriety chapter. While you are drinking hard, you tend to hang around or feel comfortable with people like you. Friends who don't probe, who are happiest with more superficial dynamics, who won't call you out on your addiction. You probably stay away from scrutiny, avoiding people who attempt to make you face your problem. When you make the decision to stop, to become sober, these relationships do not serve you, and staying in them is not only an impediment, they put you in danger of relapse. You have no choice but to let them go and form new relationships, with those who support your recovery. Many in sobriety find strength and solidarity in others who are going through recovery, too, and I would highly recommend this, definitely at the start of your recovery journey, if not for good.

But becoming sober does not have to mean the end of relationships you value. Not all marriages/

partnerships where one half is an addict are built on mutual avoidance. And for those, there is plenty of hope when it comes to building or rebuilding trust and intimacy.

Therapy is vital. Both for couples and for families as a whole. Only by talking truthfully about your feelings and owning responsibility within that safe space, where you are not judged but listened to, can you really start again with loved ones. And it is an ongoing process. Because so is sobriety. Regularly checking in with yourself and your partner or children on how you feel, working through conflict as it arises, and staying humble should become a way of life, a daily, weekly practice.

Family therapy can help with healing relationships to make a recovery easier. However, those who cannot get their friends or family to come to family therapy can still support other aspects of the recovery programme. Connections with others in recovery, such as those formed during group-therapy sessions, can boost self-esteem and help in recovery efforts. Peer support during group therapy often is a powerful tool for motivating participants in the group to make sobriety possible.

Another source of building good relationships during recovery comes from individual therapy. While patients should not have anything other than a professional connection to their therapists, the latter can offer ways for the patient to find friendships and other connections outside the recovery centre. By building new relationships during recovery, the patient begins to form a new life of sobriety that will help prevent relapse.

Aside from this, here are some basics in working through alcohol dependency in relationships, whether you are still drinking or in recovery:

- If you're in a relationship and you're either starting to drink too much or hiding a more serious habit, then as hard as it is, you need to acknowledge it. Be open with your partner, talk to them.
- If you're newly sober and part of a long-term couple, then you need to decide on some ground rules with your partner. Between you, you need to put boundaries in place. If they still want to drink, that will more than likely be triggering for you. Agree on what you are comfortable with them doing in front of you.
- You can't demand that your partner doesn't drink.
- Healthy conversation is key. Be transparent about what makes you uncomfortable.
- Fill the time you would normally drink with healthier and fulfilling pursuits.
- Be prepared for your relationship dynamic to change. Part of sobriety is self-exploration, and in some cases, this means discovering ambitions and needs you didn't realise you had.
- Seek couples counselling if the above feels

problematic. You are both adjusting to a new version of you and both of you need support.

- Sobriety sometimes means more than letting go of alcohol in your life, sadly it can also ultimately mean letting go of certain relationships. When we form relationships, a certain dynamic is sealed, and whether it's healthy or not, it forms the basis on which that relationship runs. When the dynamic changes, it can cause ruptures that never heal.

- Whatever decisions you make, keep gratitude, kindness and respect at the front of your mind.

'I understood myself only after I destroyed myself. And only in the process of fixing myself, did I know who I really was'

— Sade Andria Zabala

ONE DAY AT A TIME

So here we are, at the finale of *One for the Road*. But far from it being the end, this is just the beginning for you. Your rebirth. The start of an incredible, alcohol-free adventure. I hope that, within these pages, through sharing with you something of my life and journey, you know I have empathy for you, and I've reminded you that there are literally millions of others going through the addiction and recovery journey around the world.

You. Are. Not. Alone.

As I've said all the way through this book, there is no one way of being an alcoholic, and no one way of being in sobriety. Though the common denominator is addiction, there are myriad ways to experience that. It could well be that until you started reading this, you had no idea that you might be dependent on booze, and it's been a bit of a wake-up call. Or, if you've stuck with reading through the chapters, maybe it's made you feel uncomfortable because on some level you know that things aren't right. If it was pure pain to read through this book because your mate bought it for you as an act of intervention, then, I'm sorry, but *good*. It is only by confronting your discomfort head on that you can start to move past it, start to rebuild yourself, get on that road to your brighter, more contented future. If we do nothing but self-medicate pain and don't treat the cause, we are ensuring we never properly heal. The cliché "no pain no gain" is never truer than when it comes to kicking hardcore addiction, but boy is it worth it.

The shame around addiction is the first thing we need to kick. As complex individuals, we absorb challenge and trauma in different ways. For some, a certain set of emotional reflexes means we are able to navigate our distress, confusion, anxiety and grief without numbing the effects it has had; still has. Emotional challenges are therefore hard, but not unbearable. These fortunate folk have an early-developed layer of armour. For others, for a number of reasons beyond their control, that armour is not there. Emotional challenges are then unbearable, and very rationally we mute them, numb the nerve endings. There is no shame in that. We do the best we can with what we have. But understanding this, and developing compassion for ourselves, is our best chance of developing that armour, of strengthening, and finally realising we are worth our sobriety, we are worth fighting for it.

Throughout this book, I have included quotes from my illustrious podcast guests – each of them with a unique story to tell and a unique experience of alcohol dependence. As an ambassador and training associate for ACUK (Alcohol Change UK) and keen supporter of NACOA (National Association for Children of Alcoholics), I understand that living with a parent who drinks to excess casts as much of a shadow over your life as being an alcoholic does. The loneliness, the rejection, the abandonment and heartbreak experienced by COAs is lifelong. If they don't succumb to addiction themselves, they are still weighed down by it. I included Sarah Drage's detailed testimony in my chapter Children of Alcoholics because COAs so often feel their trauma is not important, and yet they are often trapped in the same vicious circle as a full-blown alcoholic. Bryony Gordon talks so clearly about her motivation and justification for her grey area drinking – something incredibly easy to slip into – and is proof that you can have an apparently "normal" (whatever that is) childhood and still find yourself in the grip of addiction. And I was blown away by Johnny Lawrence's experience, as the impoverished, mixed-race child of a violent, abusive parent, who contended so young with rejection on many levels, but who turned a life of basic survival into a powerful vocation to help others.

Wherever you are in the addiction/sobriety journey, asking yourself the question, 'What do I want my future to look like?' is a valuable check-in. If you're still drinking hard, you might have to think about that for a while, or you might dismiss it, because you're only able to project forward to the next drink and are deeply entrenched in the idea that it is only booze you want and need. The rest of the stuff – healthy relationship, good job, personal fulfilment, good mental and physical health might belong in some far-off recess of your brain, long forgotten, written off as not for you. When your self-esteem is driving your ambitions, everything rests on how high it is. If it's in the toilet, then your dreams will be, too.

You can have that future, it is within your grasp. Just as achieving sobriety is within your control.

For those treading the sobriety path, keep asking yourself this question and keep building on your dreams for the life you want. Keep it as your North Star, that glittering symbol of hope and growth that you're walking towards. Delve into your tailored toolbox, to find the tools for when your strength and willpower wane, when challenges and life curveballs give you the sucker punch, when your cravings hit hard.

But, and this might seem counter-intuitive, take *one day at a time*. Rushing impatiently at sobriety, eager to be "cured", is a natural impulse once you've made the decision to quit booze. But, to implement an aspect of the 12-Step method of recovery, humility is key. Make every day a reason to be grateful, and list the reasons for that gratitude, remind yourself that you are human and fallible, and acknowledge the courage it might take you not to drink. Keep that North Star of the future in your mind every day and work towards it. This is not a sprint, it is a marathon, so pace yourself, keeping yourself metaphorically hydrated through your daily self-check-ins.

Drinking can be a lonely experience, sobriety doesn't have to be. The opposite of addiction is connection, after all.

Listen and relate to my top ten podcast "One for the Road" where I interview a variety of people who share their life stories with me: check out the five-star reviews.

Follow me on Instagram – **@soberdave** where I share my ongoing alcohol-free adventure with you, posting daily inspirational tips and stories and regularly doing live interviews to help inspire you.

So, what have you got to lose?

TOGETHER, WE CAN DO THIS!

USEFUL (LIFE-SAVING) ORGANISATIONS

There is a wealth of professional, accredited help out there in the UK, for all the ways in which alcohol dependency affects you and the people you love. You never need to go through this alone, and reaching out to trained, caring organisations who can either give you individual support or direct you to the right place for it, has never been more accessible. Along with these organisations, make social media your friend by sourcing Instagram accounts and Facebook groups that provide specific support for anyone suffering with or close to alcohol addiction and mental health issues. Find the ones that feel right, that speak to you and your situation, and connect with other people like you by sharing on dedicated forums whenever you need to talk. As I've said ad infinitum in this book, you are not alone, you do not deserve or need to suffer in silence, and there are many people and services out there that really want you to succeed at sobriety. Below is some established and trusted UK organisations and facilities that provide invaluable help and support for mental health distress and addiction that you might want to check out.

Alcohol Change UK. Working for a society free from alcohol, Alcohol Change creates evidence-driven change by working towards five key changes: improved knowledge, better policies and regulation, shifted cultural norms, improved drinking behaviours, and more and better support and treatment.

www.alcoholchange.org.uk

NACOA. Established in 1990, specifically for adult children of alcoholics, NACOA (National Association for Children of Alcoholics) provides free confidential information, advice and support for anyone affected by their parent's drinking.

www.nacoa.org.uk

Alcoholics Anonymous (AA) is concerned solely with the personal recovery and continued sobriety of individual alcoholics who turn to the Fellowship for help.

www.alcoholics-anonymous.org.uk

SMART Recovery helps participants decide whether they have a problem, builds up their motivation to change and offers a set of proven tools and techniques to support recovery.

www.smartrecovery.org.uk

Al-Anon Family Groups UK & Eire is there for anyone whose life is or has been affected by someone else's drinking, with group meetings in all major towns across the UK.

www.al-anonuk.org.uk

We Are With You is a charity providing free, confidential support to people experiencing issues with drugs, alcohol or mental health.

www.wearewithyou.org.uk

The Samaritans. Available 24 hours a day, 365 days a year, the Samaritans are there to listen to you, whatever you are going through. Call the 24-hour helpline: 116 123

www.samaritans.org

CRUSE helps people through bereavement – one of the most painful times in life – with support, information and campaigning. Helpline – Mon to Fri from 9.30am to 5pm, Sat and Sun from 9.30am to 2pm.

www.cruse.org.uk

Talk to Frank confidentially provides vital information about drug use and drug abuse.

www.talktofrank.com

Turning Point works with people who need support with drug and alcohol use, mental health, offending behaviour, unemployment issues and people with a learning disability. They aim to inspire and empower them to discover new possibilities in their lives.

www.turning-point.co.uk

Mind provides support and individual advice for anyone either suffering with mental health issues themselves, or who is living with someone who does.

www.mind.org.uk

REFERENCES

https://www.nhs.uk/conditions/infertility/

https://www.nhs.uk/common-health-questions/
mens-health/how-can-i-improve-my-chances-of-
becoming-a-dad/

ACKNOWLEDGEMENTS

Big thanks to the people who have helped me with the writing of this book – Emily Thomas and Letty Butler for their hard work and passion for my vision.

To everyone throughout my sobriety journey who've supported me, shared their own unique experiences and joined my online community @soberdave – you have all kept me buoyant during the most challenging times in the past few years.

A special thanks to Sarah Drage for sharing her own personal story about her dad Steve, and for all the hard work she does to help support others in the community.

Also, thanks to Piers Jennings for craftily suggesting that I join him for three months of sobriety – it worked!

To Shaun and Lee Fennings for supporting me from the very beginning and to my therapist Richard who has always provided me with a safe, non-judgemental space, which has allowed me the opportunity to continue my journey of self-discovery.

A big thanks to Daniella Attanasio-Martinez for editing and producing my podcast to such a high standard.

33098928R00115